FRANKLIN DELANO ROOSEVELT

FRANKLIN DELANO
ROOSEVELT

RUSSELL FREEDMAN

CLARION BOOKS

New York

FRONTISPIECE: Roosevelt arrives in Chicago to accept
the Democratic nomination for president, July 1932.

Sources of photographs and prints are cited on page 195.

Clarion Books
a Houghton Mifflin Company imprint
215 Park Avenue South, New York, NY 10003

Book designed by Sylvia Frezzolini

Printed in the U.S.A.

Library of Congress Cataloging-in-Publication Data
Freedman, Russell.   Franklin Delano Roosevelt / by Russell Freedman.   p.   cm.
Summary: Photographs and text trace the life of Franklin Delano Roosevelt
from his birth in 1882 through his youth, early political career,
and presidency, to his death in Warm Springs, Georgia, in 1945.
ISBN 0-89919-379-X
1. Roosevelt, Franklin D. (Franklin Delano), 1882–1945 – Juvenile literature.
2. Presidents – United States – Biography – Juvenile literature.
[1. Roosevelt, Franklin D. (Franklin Delano), 1882–1945. 2. Presidents.]
I. Title.   E807.F736   1990
973.917′092 – dc20   89-34986
[B]   CIP
[92]   AC
H AL   10 9 8 7 6 5 4 3 2 1

◆◆

FOR ANN TROY

CONTENTS

A fireside chat. Seated at his White House desk on Sunday, March 12, 1933 — a week after taking office — President Roosevelt delivers his first radio report to the American people.

THE MAN WHO CHANGED AMERICA

"The country needs and, unless I mistake its temper, the country demands bold, persistent experimentation. It is common sense to take a method and try it. If it fails, admit it frankly and try another. But above all, try something."

FRANKLIN D. ROOSEVELT

"My friends," the voice began, "I want to speak with you tonight about a problem that concerns us all. . . ."

The voice was a familiar one. Across the country, sixty million Americans had gathered around their radios to hear Franklin Delano Roosevelt's latest report to the nation. His talks were called "fireside chats" because he spoke in such a relaxed and easy way, as though he were sitting by a cozy fireplace or on a front porch with his neighbors. The president made each listener feel that he was speaking directly to him or to her.

Years later, Eleanor Roosevelt wrote that after her husband's death, people would stop her on the street to tell her "they missed the way the president used to talk to them. They'd say, 'He used to talk to me about my government.'"

FDR has been called the first great American radio voice. He took office in 1933, during the early days of radio, and became the first chief executive to make full use of the new medium. When he was scheduled to speak, people wouldn't think of making other plans. If they did not yet own a radio set, they would walk across the street or up the road to visit friends or neighbors who did.

Roosevelt loved to be first. As a young man, he was the first political candidate in his district to campaign by automobile. Later, he was the first presidential candidate to fly in an airplane. As president, he was the first to name a woman to his cabinet, the first to appoint a press secretary, and the first to leave the country in time of war.

He was such a dynamic president, people forgot that he could not stand up without help. He could not take the smallest step without his steel leg braces and the support of crutches or someone's arm. His chief means of locomotion was a wheelchair.

Sitting at his desk, he gave the appearance of great physical strength. Through constant exercise, he had developed massive shoulders, muscular arms, and a powerful chest. Jack Dempsey, the boxing champion, said that FDR had the most impressive shoulder muscles he had ever seen. And yet Roosevelt's legs were wasted and limp, crippled by infantile paralysis, or polio.

This man who could not walk became the leader of a country paralyzed by uncertainty and despair. Not since Abraham Lincoln in 1861 had a president taken the oath of office at a more desperate moment. Lincoln was confronted with a divided nation on the verge of civil war. Roosevelt took office in the fourth year of an economic catastrophe far more destructive than any natural disaster. So many people were out of work, it was impossible to count them. Millions of families were in dire need. The nation's economy seemed ready to collapse, and Americans lived in fear.

At the worst of times, Roosevelt was able to lift people's spirits and transform the country's mood. "This nation asks for action and action now," he said in his inaugural address. "We must act quickly." And act he did, with confidence and hope.

During his twelve years in office, FDR had to meet not just one national crisis, but two. He led the American people through the Great Depression. Then, as commander in chief, he guided the nation to victory during World War II.

He was president longer than anyone else. The first and only American president to be elected to a third term, he served part of a fourth term as well. After his death, Congress adopted a constitutional amendment limiting a president to two terms.

His critics felt that even one term was too much. Roosevelt was a dangerous man, they charged, a hypocrite who would do anything to get votes. As he expanded the federal government and ran for office again and again and again, he was called a power-hungry dictator. Almost every decision he made aroused heated controversy.

Some of his most bitter enemies were members of his own moneyed class – people of wealth and privilege among whom he had grown up and lived all his life. As president, he raised their taxes, regulated their business practices, and challenged their traditional dominance of American political life. To them, he was "a traitor to his class." Many of them hated him so much, they could not stand to say his name. They called him "that man in the White House."

FDR's admirers saw an entirely different man, a magnetic leader whose warmth and optimism forged a bond with the American people. During his campaign for reelection in 1936, crowds greeted him not as a dictator but as a savior. People cried out, "He saved my home!" or "He gave me a job!" They waved hand-lettered signs reading "Thank God for Roosevelt" and "Roosevelt Is My Friend."

Even today, FDR and his policies are still being debated. But his impact on our own times is immense. The country we are living in today is to a

Roosevelt holds his Scottie dog, Fala, as he greets five-year-old Ruthie Bie, granddaughter of a caretaker at Hyde Park. This informal snapshot by FDR's cousin, Margaret Suckley, is one of the few pictures of the president in a wheelchair.

The most famous dog of his day, Fala traveled around the world with the president.

prising extent the work of Franklin Delano Roosevelt's administration.

No president has done more to change the relationship between ordinary citizens and their government. Before FDR, there was no such thing as unemployment insurance or social security in the United States. People who were old or sick or out of a job had to fend for themselves or seek help from charity. There was no bank deposit insurance, and when a bank failed, as thousands did, people lost the savings of a lifetime. There was no regulation of the stock market before FDR, no minimum wage or maximum hours, no federal guarantee of the right to join a union, no federal commitment to equal opportunity or high employment.

During Roosevelt's administration, the federal government, for the first time, made itself responsible for the welfare of those Americans who suffered economic hardship through no fault of their own. "They have a right to call upon the government for aid," he said, "and a government worthy of the name must make a fitting response."

Under FDR's leadership, the United States also assumed the responsibilities of a world power. When he came to office, America had little influence overseas. As late as 1939, the U.S. Army ranked eighteenth in the world, behind those of Romania and Spain. When Roosevelt died in 1945, World War II was almost over and America had become the most powerful nation in history. In his historic meetings with other wartime leaders, FDR helped create the United Nations and the political framework of the postwar world.

FDR dominated his era as few leaders have been able to do. Frances Perkins, his secretary of labor and one of his oldest friends, believed that the secret of Roosevelt's character was "a capacity for living and growing that remained to his dying day. It accounts for his rise from a rather unpromising young man to a great man — not merely a President, but a man who . . . will be loved as a symbol of hope and social justice long after his generation and his works have passed away."

At age one and a half, Franklin perches on his father's shoulder, holding a rose.

GROWING UP RICH

"His father and I always expected a great deal of Franklin. . . . After all, he had many advantages that other boys did not have."

SARA DELANO ROOSEVELT

As soon as he was old enough to ride, Franklin was given his own horse – a fine Welsh pony named Debby. From then on, he went with his father as they made the rounds of Springwood, the Roosevelt country estate.

Every day they rode together through fields and woods, past apple and pear orchards, past fat dairy cows grazing in the meadow. Along the way, the workmen of the estate – the coachman, grooms, and stableboys, the gardener and farmhands – tipped their hats as young Master Franklin and his father rode by.

They stopped to inspect the barns, the greenhouse, and the stables, where Franklin's father raised champion racing trotters. Then they headed back to their big clapboarded house with its staff of servants and stained-glass windows overlooking the Hudson River.

The Roosevelt estate occupied hundreds of acres of rolling farmland along the wooded bluffs of the Hudson, just south of the village of Hyde Park, New York. Franklin was born there on January 30, 1882. An only child, he knew that someday he would inherit Springwood. And he knew that his family belonged to an exclusive and privileged class. The Roosevelts had a coat of arms and a Dutch Bible that recorded more than two centuries of family births, weddings, and deaths.

The first Roosevelt in America had come over from Holland during the 1640s. On Franklin's mother's side, the Delanos traced their ancestry all the way back to the second shipload of settlers to arrive at Plymouth Colony in 1621.

Sara Delano, Franklin's mother, had grown up on a Hudson River estate not far from Hyde Park. She was twenty-six years old when she married James Roosevelt, a widower exactly twice her age. Two years later, Franklin was born, "a splendid large baby boy," his father noted in his diary. "He weighs 10 lbs., without clothes."

James Roosevelt was vice-president of several corporations, but he spent most of his time managing his property at Springwood, leading the life of a dignified country gentleman. Though old enough to be Franklin's grandfather, he enjoyed a close relationship with the boy. James taught his son how to swim and skate, how to ride a horse and handle a boat. Sometimes he overdid it. While tobogganing with Franklin one winter, "dear James sprained his knee," Sara noted, "and I had to call the men to drag him up the hill."

Franklin idolized his father, calling him "Popsy," and James in turn doted on his son. Once, when Franklin's mother felt that he should be punished for playing a nasty trick on his governess, she turned the boy over to his father. James called Franklin into his study. He looked at him sternly and said, "Consider yourself spanked."

It was Franklin's adoring, strong-willed mother who dominated his upbringing and supervised every detail of his daily life. The boy was five before he persuaded his mother to cut off his long blond curls. He was almost eight before she allowed him to wear long pants. Throughout his

The Roosevelt family on the south lawn of Springwood, their Hyde Park estate. Nine-year-old Franklin sits astride his Welsh pony, Debby. His mother holds the family dog, Monk.

life, even after he became president, his mother was always warning him to dress warmly or put on his overshoes when it rained.

Like other youngsters of his social standing, Franklin did not attend public schools. His mother taught him to read and write before he was six. Then she put him in the hands of a succession of governesses and tutors who taught him Latin, French, and German, along with history, geography, science, and arithmetic. Every moment of his day was scheduled – up at seven, breakfast at eight, lessons with his governess from nine to noon. An hour for play, then lunch and more lessons until four, when he was allowed to be on his own until supper.

He spent much of his time in the company of grown-ups. The children of millionaire neighbors and relatives would visit Springwood now and then, but often Franklin had no playmates his own age. He wasn't allowed to mingle with the Hyde Park children, whose parents worked on the great Hudson River estates. The village children were not the "right sort," his mother said. He would go into town for haircuts with his governess, but he was told not to speak to anyone.

Franklin had tennis lessons, piano lessons, and dancing lessons. When he was ten, he started a postage stamp collection that would absorb him throughout his life. He became an enthusiastic naturalist, collecting birds' nests and eggs, and recording his observations in a notebook. When he turned eleven, his father gave him a shotgun on condition that he not hunt during the nesting season and that he bag just one specimen of each kind of bird. The boy's collection of stuffed and mounted birds grew rapidly. Before he went away to school, he had shot and identified more than three hundred species native to the Hudson Valley.

He also had a passion for photography. With the tripod-mounted Kodak that was a gift from his parents, and with a self-timer, he took hundreds of photos of family members, friends, and his frequent travels.

By the time Franklin was fourteen, he had made eight trips to Europe with his parents, at a time when crossing the Atlantic meant a long voyage by ship. Of course, the Roosevelts always traveled first-class aboard the great luxury liners of the day. When they took trips in America, they also went in style. As vice-president of the Delaware & Hudson Railroad, Franklin's father was entitled to a private railroad car, the *Monon*. Its separate bed and sitting rooms were fitted out in mahogany and polished brass.

Every year, Franklin and his parents spent a long summer holiday at their seaside cottage on Campobello Island, in Canadian waters off the coast of Maine. Franklin learned to sail there. He took the helm of his father's fifty-one-foot yacht, the *Half Moon,* before he was big enough to

Franklin at eleven with his mother.

see over the top of the wheel. When he was sixteen, he was sailing his own twenty-one-foot knockabout, *New Moon*. He sailed her every day during the summer, learning to navigate the tides and currents along the rocky coast and in the Bay of Fundy.

The sea was in his blood. On his mother's side, the Delanos were whalers and merchant skippers who sailed in tall-masted clipper ships to distant ports in Europe and South America and around the Cape of Good Hope to the Orient. His grandfather, Warren Delano, had made a fortune in the China trade. In Grandpa Delano's Massachusetts house, there were ship models under glass and a model of an entire Chinese village. Up in the attic, Franklin would pore over musty, canvas-backed ships' logs that had stenciled whales in the margins.

An avid camera bug at fifteen, Franklin poses with his tripod-mounted Kodak, a gift from his parents.

Growing up, he enjoyed a secure and pampered childhood in a smiling storybook world. He was a bright, self-confident boy, affectionate and outgoing, "as cheerful as a finch," his governess said. And he was eager to please. His mother often said that she would never try to influence Franklin against his own wishes, but in her heart, she was quite sure she knew what was best for her darling boy.

Franklin learned to agree cheerfully with his mother on most things big and small, but he knew how to get around her, how to have his own way. When he wanted to skip a piano lesson, he told his governess that his hand hurt. When he didn't want to attend church services, he complained of a headache that always seemed to clear up by early afternoon. His parents called it "Franklin's Sunday headache."

He never rebelled openly, but now and again he would do something to show his spirit. At Campobello one summer, he got in trouble with some other boys for releasing all the horses in the hotel stable in the middle of the night. Another time, when he was about nine, he climbed to the top of one of his father's giant oaks at Springwood. He sat there while darkness fell, watching in gleeful silence as the servants and his worried mother called for him from far below.

Most rich boys like Franklin went away to boarding school when they were twelve. He stayed home under his mother's wing until he turned fourteen. In 1896, he entered Groton, an exclusive Massachusetts prep school, arriving with his parents in his father's private railroad car. "It is hard to leave our darling boy," Sara wrote in her diary. "James and I feel this parting very much."

Groton was modeled after the great boarding schools of England. Practically all the students came from families of wealth and social position and would go on to Ivy League colleges. At Groton, they were expected to live by strict rules, show the proper school spirit, and act like gentlemen.

Franklin was a "new boy," an outsider, since most of his classmates had entered the school and formed friendships two years earlier. Anxious to fit in and be accepted, he tried out for every activity in sight. Groton's recognized leaders were boys who excelled at team sports. At fourteen, Franklin was too short and spindly to make his mark as an athlete. He was assigned to the seventh-string football squad. When he went out for baseball, he was put on the team called the Bum Baseball Boys, or BBB, made up of the worst players in school.

The one sport in which he did well was the high kick, a game peculiar

The first and second football squads at Groton. Franklin (in white turtleneck, front row) worked his way up from the seventh squad to the second.

As manager of the Groton baseball team, Franklin poses with the players.

to Groton, which required more persistence and pluck than skill. The idea was to leap into the air and kick a tin pan suspended from the ceiling of the gym. Franklin became a champion high kicker, reaching 7 feet 3½ inches – 2 feet higher than he was – and suffering some nasty bruises when he came crashing back down to the gymnasium floor. "The whole left side of my body is sore and my left arm is a little swollen," he boasted in a letter home.

As a student, he did well enough. In his first report, he earned a respectable grade average of 7.79 out of a possible score of 10. However, he received a 9.68 for neatness and a perfect mark for punctuality. Worried that his punctuality prize would give him a bad name with the older boys, Franklin made a show of testing school discipline. He was relieved when he finally received a black mark for talking in the classroom. "I have served off my first black mark today," he told his parents, "and I am very glad I got it as I was thought to have no school spirit before."

Though he was away from home, he was never far from his mother's thoughts. When he went out for football, Sara wrote anxiously: "As your heart is a little weak, you must be sure not to overdo. It would be absolutely dangerous for you to play too hard or too long at football. I shall be glad when you begin golf instead."

Groton's founder and headmaster, the Reverend Endicott Peabody, exerted a lasting influence on Franklin. A broad-shouldered, square-jawed six-footer with piercing blue eyes and a commanding voice, Peabody ruled the school by the force of his powerful personality. The boys loved and feared him. Once, when a defiant student told the headmaster in front of the school that he had been unfair, Peabody gave the boy six black marks and reminded him that "obedience comes before all else."

Peabody often said that Groton's special mission was to develop among its students a sense of social responsibility. He told his boys that because of their wealth and privilege, they had an obligation to become leaders of American society. It was their duty to uphold the nation's ideals, and to dedicate themselves to public service. "If some Groton boys do not enter political life and do something for our land," he declared, "it won't be because they have not been urged."

A shining example of the kind of public-spirited leader that Peabody had in mind was his good friend Theodore Roosevelt, a distant cousin of Franklin's and a rising young politician who had just been appointed assistant secretary of the navy. Franklin was thrilled when "Cousin Teddy" accepted Peabody's invitation to speak at Groton. Teeth and spectacles gleaming, Theodore told his admiring audience about his recent adventures as head of the New York City police board.

A year later, in 1898, Theodore Roosevelt was elected governor of New York. "We were all wild with delight when we heard of Teddy's election," Franklin wrote home. He attended Roosevelt's inauguration in Albany with his parents.

During his four years at Groton, Franklin grew seven inches and developed an air of jaunty self-assurance. He ranked in the upper fourth of his class of nineteen boys, became one of the school's star debaters, and worked his way up from the seventh-string football squad to the second. When he failed to make the baseball team, he became team manager. He would go out early in the morning to work on the diamond, resodding the grass and marking the baselines.

In his last year, Franklin was appointed a dormitory prefect, which gave him the privilege of a private study and the responsibility of keeping order among the younger boys. He was "gray-eyed, cool, self-possessed, intelligent," one of them recalled, "and had the warmest, most friendly and understanding smile." Another classmate expressed a different opinion, saying that Franklin had "an independent, cocky manner and at times became very argumentative and sarcastic."

When he graduated, he was "rather tickled" to learn that he had won

Franklin grew seven inches at Groton, nearly reaching his full height of six feet, one and a half inches. Here he poses on the school grounds with his father. Franklin was seventeen at the time. His father was seventy.

In the senior play at Groton, a musical farce called The Wedding March, *Franklin (right) plays the role of Uncle Boppady.*

the Latin prize — a forty-volume set of Shakespeare. For the rest of his life, he would maintain a friendship with the Reverend Endicott Peabody. He would send his own sons to Groton and would speak often of the ideals of character and public service he had learned there.

And Peabody said of him: "He was a quiet, satisfactory boy, of more than ordinary intelligence, taking a good position in his Form, but not brilliant. Athletically he was rather too slight for success. We all liked him."

From Groton, Franklin went on to Harvard College, enrolling as a freshman in September 1900. "My dearest Mama and Papa," he wrote, "Here I am, in Cambridge, and in twelve hours I shall be a full registered member of the Class of 1904."

With Lathrop Brown, a classmate from Groton, he moved into a spacious two-bedroom apartment on the Mount Auburn Street "Gold Coast," the area favored by aristocratic young men who could afford to pass up the bleak dormitory rooms in Harvard Yard. Instead of eating in the common dining halls, he took his meals in an exclusive private dining hall, at a table reserved for Groton graduates — "great fun and most informal," he told his parents.

He tried out for football, but at six foot one and only 145 pounds, he was still too spindly to make the team. Instead, he played end on an intramural team. When he failed to win a place on the freshman crew, or rowing team, he made the best of it by joining a rowing club.

He also signed up as a candidate for the undergraduate daily newspaper, the *Crimson,* along with seventy rivals. Competition for jobs on the *Crimson* was keen, and the work demanded long hours. Editors were picked on the basis of dedication and ability. "If I work hard for two years I may be made an editor," Franklin wrote home. "I have to make out notices and go to interviews, so I am very busy."

The Harvard man:
"...a little studying,
a little riding, and
a few party calls."

The *Crimson* was one place at Harvard where family connections and social standing were not much help. Still, being a cousin of Theodore Roosevelt didn't hurt. Shortly after Franklin entered Harvard, Theodore was elected vice-president of the United States on a ticket headed by William McKinley.

A few months later, Franklin heard that Cousin Teddy was staying overnight at the Boston home of Harvard Professor Abbott Lowell. Hoping to see his eminent cousin, he phoned the professor's home and was put right through to the vice-president. Teddy was delighted to hear from Franklin. They could meet the next morning, he suggested, right after Lowell's nine o'clock class in constitutional government. He was planning to talk to the class about his experiences as governor of New York. The lecture was being kept a secret to hold the crowds down.

"That was a beautiful piece of news and neatest scoop in the world," Franklin recalled. The next morning a banner headline in the *Crimson* read VICE-PRESIDENT ROOSEVELT TO LECTURE IN GOVERNMENT I THIS MORNING AT 9 IN SANDERS.

By class time, hundreds of students and curiosity seekers were milling around the entrance to the lecture hall. Professor Lowell was furious, and he phoned the *Crimson* to protest. But the vice-president didn't seem to mind. And Franklin's front-page scoop helped him win election as one of five new *Crimson* editors picked at the end of the year. By then, Cousin Teddy had become president of the United States, following the assassination of William McKinley.

Franklin majored in history and government, with English and public speaking as minors, but his outside activities and a busy social life took up most of his time. With his good looks and famous name, he was much sought after by the socially prominent hostesses of Boston and Cambridge. Franklin fell into the swim easily. He bought himself evening shoes, a derby, and a new dress suit that "looked like a dream and was much admired." His weekends were filled with dinners, dances, and parties. As a scholar, he was content to squeak by, passing his courses with a "gentleman's C" and an occasional B. He told his mother that his schedule consisted of "a little studying, a little riding, and a few party calls."

He was still in his freshman year when his father died after a lingering heart ailment at the age of seventy-two. James had always been a cherished companion, and Franklin was stung by the loss. At home in Hyde Park, he did his best to comfort his grieving mother. When he finally took the train back to Harvard, she wrote, "You need not worry about me for I am all right."

Soon afterwards, Sara decided to take a place in Boston so she could be close to her son. She rented an apartment "near enough to the University to be on hand should he want me and far enough removed not to interfere in his college life."

Wearing a snappy straw boater and striped shirt, Franklin romps with friends at his uncle's country estate during the summer of 1902.

For a wealthy young man like Franklin, college life at Harvard meant entry into a network of fashionable clubs. In his sophomore year, he was elected to the Institute of 1770, which took about one-fourth of his class and was the key to membership in more exclusive clubs. Then he was invited to join Delta Kappa Epsilon, known as "Dickey," a secret fraternity reserved for Harvard's social elite. But he did not receive an invitation from Porcellian, the most exclusive and snobbish of all the clubs that signified social success at Harvard.

Franklin's father had been an honorary member of Porcellian while studying law at Harvard. Cousin Teddy had been invited to join the club as a Harvard undergraduate. But Franklin was turned down. Of course, he never knew why. Perhaps he was too anxious to join, too eager to be liked — a bit too forward for the socially conscious young men who formed the inner circle of Porcellian. Whatever the reason, Franklin learned for the first time how it feels to be snubbed by a social group. Years later he would tell a friend that his failure to make Porcellian had been "the greatest disappointment of my life."

Franklin's greatest success at Harvard turned out to be his work on the *Crimson*. As a sophomore, he was already spending six hours a day at the newspaper's grimy, ink-spattered headquarters. The following year he became an assistant managing editor, and in January 1903, he beat out his rival to become managing editor. The next step — election as "president" or editor in chief — would follow automatically. He won the post not because he was an outstanding reporter or writer, but because he was willing to put in the time and effort. As Franklin put it, he "worked like a dog."

Because he had taken advanced college-level courses at Groton, he was able to finish his Harvard course of studies in three years. He could have graduated in 1903. But in order to serve as the *Crimson*'s editor in chief, he returned to Harvard to spend his fourth year in graduate school.

The staff of The Harvard Crimson, *the undergraduate daily newspaper, 1904. Elected president and editor in chief, Roosevelt (front row, center) held the* Crimson's *top job.*

During his college years, nothing meant as much to Franklin as his work on the student newspaper. He had never been an admired athlete or brilliant scholar. He had been found wanting by Harvard's most exclusive club. But on the *Crimson*, he triumphed. As editor in chief, he served as spokesman for the entire Harvard community.

One of his fellow editors recalled that Franklin "liked people . . . and made them instinctively like him. Moreover, in his geniality there was a kind of frictionless command." Later, when Roosevelt entered public life, he would tell reporters assigned to cover him that he understood their problems because he, too, had been a newspaperman.

Franklin and his fifth cousin Eleanor were secretly engaged when they posed for this photo as members of a relative's wedding party in June 1904. Franklin was twenty-two, Eleanor nineteen. They were married the following year, on St. Patrick's Day.

THREE

LOVE AND POLITICS

*"I never had as much fun in my life
as I am having right now."*

FRANKLIN D. ROOSEVELT

"Franklin gave me quite a startling announcement," Sara Roosevelt wrote in her diary on Thanksgiving Day, 1903. Her son had just told her that he intended to marry Anna Eleanor Roosevelt, his fifth cousin once removed.

Sara was not pleased. Since her husband's death, she had looked forward to having Franklin to herself when he finished Harvard. He could study law, start a gentleman's practice, settle at Hyde Park, and become a country squire like his father. After that, there would be plenty of time to think of marriage.

Besides, Franklin was not yet twenty-two. Eleanor had just turned nineteen. In Sara's opinion, they were far too young to marry.

Back at Harvard, Franklin tried to reassure his mother. "Dearest Mama," he wrote, "I know what pain I must have caused you and you know I wouldn't do it if I really could have helped it. . . . I am the happiest man just now in the world, likewise the luckiest – And for you, dear

Mummy, you know that nothing can ever change what we have always been and always will be to each other – only now you have two children to love and to love you – and Eleanor as you know will always be a daughter to you in every true way."

Sara did not disapprove of Eleanor. She was a lovely girl, *and* a Roosevelt. Her uncle Theodore was president. Even so, Sara resisted the idea of her son's marriage. She made him promise to keep the engagement a secret until he and Eleanor had plenty of time to think it over.

Eleanor did her best to win Sara's blessing. "It is impossible for me to tell you how I feel toward Franklin," she wrote. "I know just how you feel and how hard it must be, but I do so want you to learn to love me a little."

As distant cousins, Eleanor and Franklin had known each other since childhood. While growing up, they met from time to time at family parties, and Franklin once told his mother that "Cousin Eleanor has a very good mind." But it wasn't until Franklin's senior year at Harvard that their friendship blossomed into romance.

In many ways, they were opposites. Franklin was handsome and debonair, an exuberant young man who wore his easy charm and stylish clothes with an air of breezy self-assurance. He seemed to feel as though he could do anything. Eleanor was shy and retiring, an intensely serious young woman with a solemn manner and prominent teeth who once described herself as "an ugly duckling."

Franklin's secure and happy childhood had given him all the self-confidence in the world. Eleanor's childhood had been painful. Her beautiful mother, Anna Hall Roosevelt, seemed cold and distant to the little girl. She died of diphtheria when Eleanor was eight. Her father was Theodore Roosevelt's younger brother, Elliott. Eleanor adored her father. But he was away from home most of the time. He died from the effects of alcoholism when she was ten.

Eleanor was raised by her stern and disapproving Grandmother Hall. She was always "afraid of being scolded, afraid that other people would not like me." When she was fifteen, she was sent to Allenswood, a boarding school for girls in England, where she made lifelong friendships and spent "the happiest years of my life." She wanted to stay longer, but after three years her grandmother summoned her back to New York to make her formal debut into society. Eleanor said later that "by no stretch of the imagination could I fool myself into thinking I was a popular debutante." For her, the social scene was "utter agony."

In January 1903, she was one of the guests invited to Franklin's twenty-first birthday party at Hyde Park. They began to see each other at dinners and dances in Hudson River mansions and Manhattan townhouses. That summer, Franklin invited Eleanor to visit his family's summer place on Campobello Island.

He found himself drawn to her. While people said that Eleanor was no beauty, many men found her attractive. She was tall and willowy with beautiful skin and luxuriant golden hair. Her blue eyes shone with intelligence, and she had an inner strength that Franklin seemed to find reassuring. "The first summer at Campo I saw most clearly how Franklin admired you," a friend told her.

At first, Eleanor could not believe that someone like Franklin was interested in her. But as she came to trust him, she opened her heart. They took long walks in the woods at Campobello, picnicked on cliffs overlooking the sea, and read to each other by firelight. Franklin could always make her laugh. He was kind and thoughtful.

That autumn in New York, he began to call for Eleanor at the Rivington Street Settlement House on the Lower East Side, where she had volunteered to teach dancing and calisthenics to poor immigrant children. One afternoon a child fell ill. Franklin helped take the ailing girl home, carrying her up the narrow tenement stairs and down the dark, rancid hallway to her parents' apartment. "He was absolutely shaken when he saw the cold water tenement where the child lived," Eleanor recalled, "and kept saying he simply could not believe human beings lived that way."

On the weekend of November 21, 1903, Franklin invited Eleanor to the Harvard-Yale football game in Cambridge. The day after the game he proposed, and Eleanor said yes. He recorded the event in his diary, in a private code he knew his mother could not decipher: "After lunch I have a never to be forgotten walk to the river with my darling."

Franklin's mother had asked them to keep their engagement a secret, and they did so for almost a year. By then, Sara had reconciled herself to the marriage. "I must try to be unselfish," she told her son, "& of course my dear child I *do* rejoice in your happiness, & shall not put any stones or straws ever in the way of it."

In January 1905, Franklin entered Columbia Law School, choosing it instead of Harvard so he could be near Eleanor in New York. Two months later, on Saint Patrick's Day, they were married in the parlor of a New York City townhouse owned by a cousin of Eleanor's. The wedding was performed by Franklin's old headmaster, the Reverend Endicott Peabody. And the bride was given in marriage by her uncle, Theodore Roosevelt, president of the United States. "Well, Franklin," said the president afterwards, "there's nothing like keeping the name in the family."

That summer, after Franklin's first term at law school, the couple left for a belated honeymoon, a three-month grand tour of Europe. When they sailed back to New York, a townhouse on fashionable East Thirty-sixth Street was waiting for them. It had been rented, furnished, and staffed with three servants by Franklin's mother.

Their first child, Anna, was born in May 1906 – eight months after they returned from their honeymoon. Anna was followed by James in 1907; the first Franklin, Jr., who died soon after his birth in 1909; Elliott

Family portrait. By 1908, Eleanor and Franklin had their first two children—baby James and two-year-old Anna.

in 1910; the second Franklin, Jr., in 1914; and John in 1916. For the first twelve years of her marriage, Eleanor said, she was "always getting over a baby or having one."

Meanwhile, Franklin's mother had built two adjoining townhouses on

East Sixty-fifth Street – one for herself, the other as "A Christmas present to Franklin and Eleanor from Mama." The twin houses were connected by sliding doors. In the fall of 1908, they all moved in together.

Franklin had passed his bar exams in the spring of 1907. He went to work for a prominent Wall Street law firm, Carter, Ledyard, and Milburn. He was expected to serve a year's apprenticeship as an unpaid law clerk. Of course, money was not a problem. Franklin and Eleanor had both inherited large trust funds. Between them, they had an income of about twelve thousand dollars a year, a substantial amount at a time when a male schoolteacher earned about five hundred dollars a year.

They spent weekends at Hyde Park and summer holidays at Campobello. Franklin knew that he could look forward to a comfortable partnership in his law firm, but he was bored. He was already talking about entering politics. He told his fellow clerks that he wasn't going to practice law forever. He intended to run for office at the first opportunity. He wanted to follow in the footsteps of his cousin Teddy, who had risen from the New York State legislature to the White House.

His chance came in 1910, when Democratic leaders from his own Dutchess County invited Franklin to run for the New York State Senate from the Twenty-sixth District, an area that included Hyde Park. Like his father, Franklin was a registered Democrat. Yet the Twenty-sixth District was solidly Republican. Franklin was offered the nomination because he came from a prominent local family and was wealthy enough to finance his own campaign. But no one thought he could win.

Made up of Columbia, Dutchess, and Putnam counties, the Twenty-sixth District stretched for ninety miles along the eastern bank of the Hudson. Franklin wanted to meet as many voters as possible. To do so, he became the first political candidate in the region to campaign by automobile. He rented the only automobile in the area – a bright red, two-

*Campaigning for a seat in the New York State Senate in 1910, Roosevelt visited
every corner of his election district, traveling by rented car and by train.
Eleanor usually went with him. Here they wait beside the railroad tracks at
a tiny hamlet in upstate New York.*

cylinder Maxwell touring car with brass headlamps but no windshield or
top. Then he teamed up with the Democratic candidates for the state
assembly and for Congress and set out on the campaign trail. With American flags flapping from its hood and fenders, the Maxwell bounced and
sputtered over rutted country roads, frightening horses and cattle, stopping at every crossroads village and country store.

At each stop, the candidates made speeches, shook hands, and chatted with the local farmers and townsfolk. Though he had been a star debater at Groton, Franklin had never faced an audience of real voters. The first time Eleanor heard him speak, she thought he seemed "high strung and at times, nervous. . . . He spoke slowly, and every now and then there would be a long pause, and I would be worried for fear that he would never go on."

Averaging ten speeches a day during the month-long campaign, Franklin quickly improved his speaking style. He learned to greet each crowd with the opening line, "My friends," to say something nice about the town he was in, and to talk about local issues. He promised to be independent, to support government reform, and to defend the interests of the district's many farmers.

The twenty-eight-year-old candidate addresses voters in Dutchess County, New York.

By election day, he had traveled some two thousand miles over country roads in the Maxwell, despite blowouts and breakdowns. He won an upset victory, beating his Republican opponent by more than a thousand votes.

Before he even took his seat in the state senate, the twenty-eight-year-old freshman lawmaker was one of the best-known political figures in New York. Thirty years earlier, his cousin Theodore had also started his career in the state legislature. Franklin was regarded as Teddy's political heir. As soon as he arrived in Albany, newspaper reporters rushed to interview him. "He is tall and lithe," said the *New York Times*. "With his handsome face and his form of supple strength he could make a fortune on the stage."

He stepped quickly into the limelight. Shortly after taking office, Roosevelt found himself in the midst of a noisy political battle. He joined a group of rebellious Democrats who defied party discipline and challenged Tammany Hall, the powerful organization, or "machine," that controlled Democratic politics in New York. At the time, U.S. senators were elected by state legislatures, not by popular vote. Roosevelt and his fellow rebels refused to support Tammany's handpicked candidate for the senate. They declared that they were "fighting against the boss rule system."

Many old-timers dismissed Roosevelt as a "college kid" trying to attract attention. He was called a "snob," a "political prig" who knew little about the real world. "Awful arrogant fellow, that Roosevelt," said Big Tim Sullivan, Tammany's Boss of the Bowery.

But Franklin had tasted the thrill of political combat. "There is nothing I love as much as a good fight," he told a reporter. "I never had as much fun in my life as I am having right now."

Newspapers across the country featured the fight that this new Roosevelt was making against bossism and machine politics. But when it came

State Senator Roosevelt at his desk in Albany, 1911. He is wearing his pince-nez —eyeglasses that clip to the bridge of the nose.

to the everyday business of the state senate, Franklin failed to impress the progressives who were working to correct social abuses — low wages, long hours, bad housing, child labor, and unsanitary working and living conditions.

One of the leading reformers of the day was a young woman named Frances Perkins. She had come to Albany to lobby for a bill that would limit the working week of women to fifty-four hours. Roosevelt was hesitant about the bill, which was opposed by farmers in his district. Canneries employed large numbers of women. Farmers feared that a shorter workweek would slow down cannery operations and reduce the demand for farm products. Roosevelt finally voted in favor of the bill, but he hadn't pushed for it. Frances Perkins felt that he had little understanding of the problems faced by ordinary working people. "I took it hard that a young man who had so much spirit did not do so well in this," she recalled. "I have a vivid picture of him operating on the floor of the Senate, tall and slender, very active and alert . . . rarely smiling, with an unfortunate habit — so natural that he was unaware of it — of throwing his head up. This, combined with his pince-nez and great height, gave him the appearance of looking down his nose at most people."

When Roosevelt faced reelection in 1912, he fell ill with typhoid fever and was too sick to campaign. He hired Louis Howe, a seasoned Albany newspaper reporter, to handle his campaign for him. While Franklin lay flat on his back in bed, Howe flooded the Twenty-sixth District with campaign letters, pamphlets, and ads. Roosevelt was popular with the farmers in his district. He won his second term without making a single personal appearance.

Howe hadn't thought much of Roosevelt at first, calling him a "spoiled silk-pants sort of guy." But he had come to admire Franklin's independence and fighting spirit. "The boy's got courage," he said. Howe decided that young Roosevelt had a bright political future. He became one of Franklin's closest friends and advisers, and his chief political aide.

Roosevelt had barely started his second term when opportunity knocked again. During the 1912 presidential campaign, he had supported Woodrow Wilson, a progressive Democrat and an advocate of political reform. Wilson knew about Roosevelt's battle with Tammany Hall. When he was elected president, he offered the young lawmaker a post as assistant secretary of the navy.

Nothing could have pleased Franklin more. "All my life I have loved ships and been a student of the Navy," he said. "The assistant secretaryship is the one place, above all others, I would love to hold."

He had been in politics less than three years, and now he was moving forward again in his cousin Teddy's footsteps. On March 17, 1913 – Franklin's eighth wedding anniversary – he was sitting at Theodore Roosevelt's old desk in the Navy Department.

"I am baptized, confirmed, sworn in, vaccinated – and somewhat at sea!" the new secretary wrote to his mother. "For over an hour I have been signing papers. . . . I will have to work like a new turbine to master this job."

Barely thirty-one years old, Roosevelt was half the age of some of the admirals he would work with. As assistant secretary, he rated a seventeen-gun salute when he visited a ship, four guns more than a rear admiral with thirty years of service. He became a familiar figure to officers and men alike as he inspected ships and shore stations, climbing into the rigging and crawling through engine spaces. "I get my fingers into everything and there's no law against it," he said.

When one of the navy's primitive submarines sank with all hands aboard, Roosevelt displayed his confidence in the new weapon by immediately going out in another submarine.

He was known as a tireless worker who would listen to advice, make decisions, cut through red tape, and get things done. "He had a tremendous vitality," his friend William Phillips recalled, "an eagerness and interest in everything, and he certainly made a very effective assistant secretary of the Navy."

When war broke out in Europe in 1914, Germany's aggressive submarine warfare in the Atlantic convinced Roosevelt that the United States must become involved. Testifying before Congress, he urged that the nation build up its armed forces. Meanwhile, he stepped up the flow of supplies to naval bases and plants. He did such a thorough job that President Wilson called him to a conference with the army chief of staff and said: "I'm very sorry, Franklin, but you've cornered the market for supplies. You'll have to divide up with the Army."

As assistant secretary of the navy, Roosevelt climbs the rigging of a naval vessel cruising off Old Point Comfort, Virginia, October 1913.

On April 6, 1917, the United States did enter World War I, joining Great Britain and France in their struggle against Imperial Germany. "The world must be made safe for democracy," President Wilson told Congress. For the first time in history, American soldiers prepared to fight in Europe.

Roosevelt plunged into the task of mobilizing the navy for wartime duty. By the end of the war, the navy's strength had climbed from sixty-five thousand officers and men to nearly half a million – including eleven thousand "yeomanettes," the first women ever to serve in naval ranks. The number of ships in commission increased from 197 to 2,003.

Roosevelt was brimming over with plans and projects to boost naval effectiveness. He was willing to try almost anything. If an idea didn't work out, he would simply drop it and go on to something else. "He was a great trial and error guy," said Admiral Emory S. Land.

One of his pet projects was a scheme to lay a wall of underwater mines across the North Sea, stretching 250 miles from Scotland to Norway. The mines would be a barrier against German submarines that ventured into the Atlantic to attack British and American ships. Naval experts said that the plan was impractical. They estimated that four hundred thousand mines would be needed to keep the U-boats bottled up in their North Sea ports.

But Roosevelt was convinced that somehow the project could be made to work. His persistence paid off when an inventor came to him with an idea: the mines could be equipped with long copper antennas that would reach out into the water and act as triggers. When a U-boat brushed against the tip of an antenna, it would set off a chain of underwater explosions. By the end of the war, some seventy thousand antenna mines, each containing three hundred pounds of TNT, had been sown under Roosevelt's direction, disrupting the passage of German submarines and limiting their effectiveness. Admiral William Sims called the mine barrage "one of the wonders of the war."

In the summer of 1918, Roosevelt sailed to Europe to tour the war zone. He inspected naval installations and visited battlefields in France and Belgium, getting close to the actual fighting. Once he came under German artillery fire. He would never forget the scene of horror and devastation he witnessed at the French fortress of Verdun, where nearly half a million men had been killed on the battlefield.

An early advocate of military air power, Roosevelt inspects a U.S. naval air station in France during World War I.

Assistant Navy Secretary Roosevelt reviews a contingent of yeomanettes, the first women ever to serve in the navy's ranks, April 1919.

Back home, he wanted to volunteer for active duty. He asked President Wilson to reassign him as a naval officer, but by then it was too late for active service. On November 11, 1918, the Armistice was signed and "the war to end all wars" was over.

The following summer Roosevelt attended the peace conference at Versailles, France, as a representative of the Navy Department. Like President Wilson, he was convinced that the United States should join the newly created League of Nations. His firsthand look at European battle-fields had impressed him with the need for an international organization to maintain world peace.

Membership in the League was a controversial issue that had deeply divided the American people. After a brutal world war, many Americans believed that the United States should stay out of Europe's affairs. They wanted no part of an international organization. And that was the view-point that prevailed. After a long and bitter debate, the U.S. Senate re-fused to approve the Versailles peace treaty ending World War I. As a result, the United States did not become a member of the League of Na-tions.

Roosevelt had never lost sight of his political goals. In 1914, New York State held its first direct primary election for U.S. senator, a reform Franklin had supported. He took a leave from the Navy Department to seek the Democratic nomination as an anti-Tammany candidate. He lost. The defeat taught him that he could not defy a powerful organization like Tammany Hall and expect to carry New York State in an election. Quietly, Roosevelt began to patch up his quarrel with his former political enemies. Never again would he openly oppose Tammany Hall.

In 1920, he entered national politics. The Democrats had nominated Governor James M. Cox of Ohio for president, and Cox picked Franklin Roosevelt as his running mate. Though he was only thirty-eight years old, Franklin had earned a fine reputation at the Navy Department. As a New Yorker, he would add geographical balance to a ticket headed by a mid-westerner. And Cox believed that the Roosevelt name still had political magic.

In those days, vice-presidential candidates usually stayed on the side-lines. Roosevelt broke with this tradition. He barnstormed across the country in a special railroad car, visiting thirty-two states and making

As Democratic candidate for vice-president in 1920, Roosevelt campaigns in Dayton, Ohio, with his running mate, James Cox.

more than a thousand speeches – the most extensive campaign ever waged by a candidate for national office. Women were voting for the first time in 1920, and Eleanor joined her husband on the campaign trail. She appeared, smiling by his side, wherever he spoke.

Cox and Roosevelt made the League of Nations the central issue of their campaign. They urged the voters to support American membership in the League. The Republican candidates, Warren G. Harding and Calvin Coolidge, opposed the League. They promised the voters "a return to normalcy" – no more reforms at home, no further entanglements in foreign affairs. After the wartime years of rationing and sacrifice, and after three hundred thousand American casualties in Europe, the American people were more interested in peace and prosperity than in high-sounding talk about international cooperation. Harding and Coolidge won by a landslide, getting 61 percent of the popular vote and carrying thirty-seven of the forty-eight states.

Roosevelt did not regard the election as a personal defeat. The campaign had taken him across America. He had talked and listened to ranchers in Wyoming, farmers in Kansas, factory workers in Chicago, sharecroppers in Alabama, longshoremen in San Francisco. "I got to know the country as only a candidate for office or a traveling salesman can get to know it," he said. He had become a skilled campaigner and a polished speaker. In ten years of public life, he had expanded his horizons, rising from a state senator concerned with three rural counties to a national figure, a leading spokesman for the Democratic party.

"The moment of defeat," he told a friend, "is the best time to lay plans for future victories."

Waving to a friend, Roosevelt strides down a Washington, D.C., street, July 1920.

DR. ROOSEVELT

*"Suddenly, there he was flat on his back,
with nothing to do but think."*

LOUIS HOWE

During his years at the Navy Department, Roosevelt was admired for his boundless energy, his charm and good looks. A friend described him as a man "breathing health and virility."

Frances Perkins remembered the impression Roosevelt made at the Democratic National Convention in San Francisco in 1920, when he was nominated for vice-president. "Tall, strong, handsome, and popular, he was one of the stars of the show," she wrote. "I recall how he displayed his athletic ability by vaulting over a row of chairs to get to the speaker's platform in a hurry."

Franklin and Eleanor led a busy social life. The lights burned late in their rented Washington house as visitors came and went. "He had a good time," said Frances Perkins. "He knew everybody, played hard, and worked as well. . . . His habit of looking down his nose was greatly modified now — it was hardly noticeable. The toss of the head up and back was softened — it had become a gesture of cheerfulness, not arrogance. He smiled when he did it."

Franklin, his mother, Sara, and Eleanor sit on the steps of their summer cottage at Campobello with the five Roosevelt children: (left to right) Elliott, Franklin, Jr., John, Anna, and James.

Franklin's children worshiped him. He was always eager to romp with them on the floor and carry them about on his shoulders, to take them riding at Hyde Park and sailing at Campobello. Like his own father, Franklin wasn't good at disciplining his children. He loved to indulge them, but when they were bad, he left the punishment to Eleanor. And as his career made greater demands on his time, he was often away from home or too busy to give his youngsters the time and attention they craved.

Early in their marriage, Eleanor left the limelight to her husband. When their first child was born, she gave up her social work. Franklin's mother insisted on it. She feared that by working with poor children, Eleanor might bring the diseases of the slums into the household.

At times, Eleanor resented her mother-in-law's interference. Sara chose the toys and clothing for her five grandchildren. She hired and fired nurses and governesses. Her New York townhouse was connected to Eleanor and Franklin's by doors that were never locked. Her summer cottage at Campobello stood just down the beach from theirs. And she was the one who owned Springwood, the house at Hyde Park where Franklin grew up. When the Roosevelts retired to its book-lined living room after dinner, Franklin sat in one of two massive carved chairs that flanked the fireplace. His mother sat in the other. "I sat anywhere," Eleanor recalled.

It was customary for the wives and children of Washington officials to spend the summer in some cooler place. Eleanor and her brood would escape to Campobello. Franklin joined them when he could, but often he stayed behind to attend to business. "I really can't stand the house all alone without you," he wrote to Eleanor. "It seems years since you left and I miss you horribly and hate the thought of the empty house."

In 1918, when Franklin returned from his tour of the European war zone, Eleanor discovered that he was having a romance with an attractive young woman named Lucy Mercer. Lucy had once worked as Eleanor's social secretary. Later she joined the Navy Department as a yeomanette. Eleanor was shocked. "The bottom dropped out of my world," she told a friend. "I faced myself, my surroundings, my world, honestly for the first time."

They discussed divorce. But in those days, divorce was scandalous. In Sara Roosevelt's eyes, a divorce was *unthinkable*. She told her son that for the sake of his children, his career, and the Roosevelt name, he must keep his family together.

"It wasn't just Sara," their son Elliott wrote, "it was Louis Howe going back and forth and just reasoning, convincing father that he had no political future if he did this. . . . Father wanted to give it up and mother felt

Lucy Mercer.

betrayed . . . but she came around because Louis convinced her. He said she could not destroy Franklin's goal and he convinced her that she too would have a great role to play. He convinced her it was better for the children."

Eleanor and Franklin were reconciled, but their relationship would never again be the same. Eleanor moved out from under her husband's shadow to create a life and identity of her own. Franklin seemed to realize how much pain he had caused her, and from then on, he tried to make amends.

For the rest of their lives, their marriage was more like a partnership based on mutual interests and a shared past. "It became a very close and very intimate partnership of great affection – never in a physical sense, but in a tremendously mental sense," said Elliott. "But there were very few light moments. . . . They never enjoyed *anything* in the way of light-heartedness in their lives."

After the 1920 presidential campaign, Roosevelt returned to New York and private life. He formed a law partnership, the firm of Emmet, Marvin, and Roosevelt. And he took a position as vice-president in charge of the New York office of the Fidelity & Deposit Company, a large bonding firm.

It was an ideal arrangement. He spent his mornings working for Fidelity & Deposit. Then he walked across the street to spend his afternoons at his Wall Street law office.

Meanwhile, he kept his name before the public. He helped organize the Woodrow Wilson Foundation, led a fund-raising drive for the Lighthouse for the Blind, and served as president of the Greater New York Boy Scouts Council. With the help of his full-time aide, Louis Howe, he issued political statements and corresponded with Democratic leaders all over the country.

Franklin and Eleanor on the beach at Campobello.

Weekends were spent at Hyde Park, summer holidays at Campobello. One afternoon during the summer of 1921, Franklin was out sailing with some of the children when they saw smoke rising from a nearby island. They went ashore, found a grove of spruce trees burning, and began to fight the fire, beating back flames with evergreen branches until the blaze was brought under control. Grimy from soot and smoke and smarting from spark burns, they sailed back to Campo. When they reached their own island, they went swimming in a freshwater lagoon, jogged two miles across the island in their wet bathing suits, then plunged into the icy waters of the Bay of Fundy for a final dip. After that, they raced back to the house.

Franklin sat on the porch and started to read the day's batch of newspapers. Then he felt a chill. His muscles began to ache. "I'd never felt that way before," he said later. Too tired to dress for dinner, he went to bed early.

The next morning, as he climbed out of bed, his left leg felt numb. "I tried to persuade myself that this trouble with my leg was muscular, that it would disappear as I used it," he said. "But presently, it refused to work, and then the other."

A doctor was summoned. He diagnosed a heavy cold, but soon it became obvious that Franklin's condition was worse than that. Stabbing pains spread through his legs and back, then crept into his shoulders, arms, and fingers. He was running a high fever. His hands were so weak that he could not hold a pen. "I don't know what's wrong with me, Louis," he said to his aide. "I just don't know."

Another doctor was called in from Bar Harbor, Maine. He prescribed deep massage. Eleanor began to sleep on a cot in her husband's sickroom, bathing him, feeding him, taking turns with Louis Howe as they massaged his limp legs for hours at a time and tried to keep up his spirits.

Finally, a specialist arrived from Boston. He found that Roosevelt was

As president of the Greater New York Boy Scouts Council, Roosevelt (far left) visits a Scout encampment at Bear Mountain, New York, July 27, 1921. This is the last photo that shows him walking unassisted.

a victim of poliomyelitis – commonly known as infantile paralysis, or polio. At the time, polio was probably the most dreaded disease in America. It struck most often at children. It could paralyze a person's arms or legs or entire body. Many victims died. And in 1921, when Roosevelt was stricken, no one knew what caused the disease or how to treat it. (The Salk vaccine against polio was not developed until 1955.)

For several weeks, Franklin lay on his sickbed in agony and fear, paralyzed from the waist down. At first, he gave in to "utter despair." But he would not abandon hope, and after a while he was able to keep up a brave front, laughing and joking with Eleanor and Louis and with the doctors who stood helplessly by his bedside.

He managed a smile for his children as they peered fearfully into the upstairs room where the shades were always drawn. "We children were allowed only a few glimpses of him, a hurried exchange of words from a doorway," James remembered. "Yet from the beginning . . . Father was unbelievably concerned about how *we* would take it. He grinned at us, and he did his best to call out, or gasp out, some cheery response to our tremulous, just-this-side-of-tears greetings."

In September, Roosevelt was transferred to a hospital in New York City. His doctor was optimistic, telling reporters, "I cannot say how long Mr. Roosevelt will be kept in the hospital, but you can say definitely that he will not be crippled." But there was no improvement. Roosevelt's legs were paralyzed. The doctors were worried that he might never sit up again, let alone stand or walk.

That autumn, as he lay in his hospital room, Franklin resolved that he would not allow himself to remain helpless. Every day he spent hours concentrating on his paralyzed muscles. Eyes closed, sweat beading on his forehead, he would concentrate on the muscles in his legs, the muscles in his feet, the muscles in his toes. He concentrated with all his might as he tried to move his big toe.

When he was discharged from the hospital in October, he told a friend, "I'll be walking on crutches in a few weeks. The doctors say there is no question but that by this spring, I will be walking without any limp."

At home, he joked about his illness with his children. He would discuss his condition with them, throw back the covers and show them his legs. He taught them the names of the muscles, and which ones he was work-

Three years after he was stricken with polio, Roosevelt stands upright with the helping hands of his valet (left) and his physician, Dr. William McDonald.

ing hardest on at that moment. "He would give us progress reports as a little life returned to various areas, and we would cheer jubilantly, as if at a football game, when Pa would report, say, a slight improvement in the muscles leading from the *gluteus maximus*," James recalled. "How we loved to talk about Pa's *gluteus maximus*."

In February 1922, Roosevelt was fitted with the leather and steel leg braces he would wear for the rest of his life. They reached from his hips to his feet. Each brace weighed seven pounds and locked at the knee, turning his limp legs into rigid stilts. With the braces and with crutches, he started the painful task of learning to walk.

At first he would tip over. His armpits became inflamed from the crutches. To strengthen his arms and shoulders, he exercised for hours every day on a pair of parallel bars.

He practiced walking, pushing his crutches ahead of him one after the other, swiveling his hips, and thrusting his legs forward as he inched ahead. His goal was to make it all the way from the house at Hyde Park to the Post Road, a quarter of a mile away. Every day he would try to make it just a bit farther down the gravel driveway. When he tipped over and fell, he could not get up by himself. He had to wait until someone came along to help him. Then he would set out again the next day, saying, "I must get down the driveway today – all the way down the driveway."

Roosevelt would never again walk by himself without the support of his braces and crutches. Never again would he race his children back to the house, beat them on the tennis court, lead them on cliff walks and cross-country hikes. Now he had to depend on others for the most ordinary tasks of everyday life. He could not dress or undress himself, get in or out of a car, go up or down steps without help. He could not bend down to pick up something he had dropped. Often he had to be lifted like a baby and carried. Yet he refused to pity himself. When a reporter came to interview him, Roosevelt said, "Now I don't want any sob stuff."

He learned to joke about his handicap. "That's funny as a crutch," he would say, throwing up his head and flashing a grin. Sometimes he would finish a conversation by saying, "Goodbye, I've got to run."

He became an authority on polio, reading everything he could find on the disease, discussing it endlessly with his doctors. And he continued to exercise, like an athlete training for the Olympics. He developed muscular arms and shoulders, and the powerful neck and chest of a weight lifter. But the muscles of his legs continued to waste away, until they hung from his massive torso as limp and lifeless as the legs of a rag doll.

Roosevelt rarely spoke about the pain and suffering he had endured. But if he kept his innermost thoughts to himself, those who knew him best did speak of his ordeal and its impact on his life.

"Suddenly, there he was flat on his back, with nothing to do but think," Louis Howe wrote. "His thoughts expanded, his horizon widened. He began to see the other fellow's point of view. He thought of others who were ill and afflicted and in want. He dwelt on many things which had not bothered him much before. Lying there, he grew bigger day by day."

Before his illness, most things had come easily to him. Now he knew what it was like to be helpless, to be weak, to be dependent on others through no fault of your own.

Frances Perkins had first known Roosevelt as a brash and self-centered young state legislator. She believed he experienced "a spiritual transformation" that purged the "slightly arrogant attitude" he displayed before. "The man emerged completely warm hearted, with humility of spirit and with a deeper philosophy," she said. "Having been to the depths of trouble, he understood the problems of people in trouble."

Eleanor felt that Franklin's illness taught him patience. He had always been restless, a man who could never sit still. Now he had learned to concentrate on one thing at a time. And he had learned to wait for results. "If you have spent two years in bed trying to wiggle your big toe," he said, "everything else seems easy."

In the end, he was so successful in shouldering aside his handicap and leading an active life, he gave the impression that he had no disability. Years later, when he became president, many Americans did not fully realize that Franklin Roosevelt could not use his legs.

As Roosevelt struggled to walk, his wife and his mother were battling over his future. Sara was sure she knew what was best for Franklin. She believed that his career was finished, that he should retire to the comfortable privacy of Hyde Park.

Eleanor rebelled. For the first time, she openly defied her mother-in-law. She would not allow Franklin to be treated like a lifelong invalid. He must remain active, she insisted. As far as possible, he must lead a normal life.

Eleanor and Sara argued bitterly and often during the first months of Franklin's illness, arguments that left Eleanor trembling with rage and Sara stiff with indignation. Once Eleanor was so angry that she blocked the doorway linking their New York townhouses by moving a heavy breakfront against it. She described those months as "the most trying period of my life."

Eleanor found an ally in Louis Howe. Together they urged Franklin to return to public life. With Howe's help, Franklin issued statements on important issues and kept up his correspondence with political leaders. Eleanor, meanwhile, began to speak on her husband's behalf at conferences and conventions, before women's groups and parent-teacher associations.

In 1922, a year after he was stricken, Roosevelt returned to work at the Fidelity & Deposit Company. He would begin his day by seeing Howe and other visitors while he had breakfast in bed. Then his chauffeur would drive him to his office in lower Manhattan and help him out of the car. Gripping his crutches, he would make his way across the sidewalk, into the building, and over the polished marble floor of the lobby, nodding and smiling to people he knew.

By 1924, he was ready for an active role in politics again. That year, Governor Alfred E. Smith of New York was a leading contender for the presidential nomination. Roosevelt admired Smith's progressive record as governor. He agreed to act as chairman of his presidential campaign. Then he was asked to place Smith's name in nomination at the Democratic National Convention in New York. It would be Roosevelt's first public speech since his illness, a chance to show that he had overcome his affliction. The energetic young man who had vaulted over a row of chairs at the Democratic convention four years earlier would now have to enter the convention hall on crutches.

Sixteen-year-old Jimmy Roosevelt never forgot the night in Madison Square Garden when he escorted his father to the speaker's platform: "As we walked – struggled, really – down the aisle to the rear of the platform, he leaned heavily on my arm, gripping me so hard it hurt. It was hot, but the heat in the building did not alone account for the perspiration which beaded on his brow. His hands were wet. His breathing was labored. Leaning on me with one arm, working a crutch with the other, his legs locked stiffly in his braces, he went on his awkward way."

As they appeared on the platform, cheers and applause rippled through the crowd. Roosevelt turned to his son, released his grip on Jimmy's arm, and slid his second crutch under his own arm. He started forward, swinging himself toward the rostrum. Now the crowd was hushed, watching silently as each crutch stabbed the platform floor.

Reaching the rostrum, Roosevelt pushed his crutches aside. He gripped the rostrum on either side, bracing himself. Standing in the spotlight's glare, he tossed back his head and flashed the famous Roosevelt grin.

Pandemonium swept through the auditorium. The cheering lasted several minutes before Roosevelt could quiet the crowd and speak:

"I ask you in all seriousness . . . to keep first in your hearts and minds the words of Abraham Lincoln – 'With malice toward none, and charity for all.'" Everything he had learned about public speaking, every trick of the trade, went into his speech that night. He spoke with moving eloquence about Al Smith, pacing himself, pausing for effect, stirring the

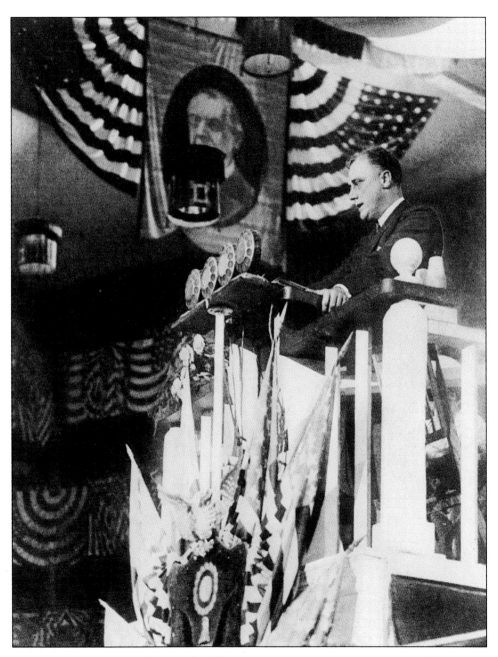

In his first public speech since his illness, Roosevelt nominates Al Smith for president at Madison Square Garden, June 26, 1924.

crowd as he praised the governor and called him the "Happy Warrior of the political battlefield," a name that would stick with Smith from then on.

The speech brought the cheering delegates to their feet in a frenzy of excitement. "No matter whether Governor Smith wins or loses, Franklin D. Roosevelt stands out as the real hero of the Democratic Convention of 1924," said the *New York Herald Tribune*.

As it turned out, Smith lost the nomination. The winner needed 732 votes, a two-thirds majority. On the 103rd ballot, the delegates finally nominated John W. Davis for president, and in the general election that fall, Davis was defeated overwhelmingly by the Republican candidate,

On crutches at Hyde Park, Roosevelt greets John W. Davis (center), who won the Democratic presidential nomination in 1924, and Al Smith, who lost it.

Calvin Coolidge. But the convention had marked a triumphant political comeback for Franklin Roosevelt.

"He has the most magnetic personality of any individual I have ever met," said Tom Pendergast, the Democratic political boss of Kansas City, "and I predict he will be the candidate on the Democratic ticket in 1928."

Throughout the 1920s, Roosevelt continued to believe that he would walk again. He had discovered that water was a wonderful therapy, and he would swim and exercise several times a week in a Hyde Park neighbor's heated indoor pool. Then he heard about Warm Springs, a rundown resort in the hills of western Georgia. Polio victims reported that they had been helped by exercising in the warm and soothing mineral waters of the resort's swimming pool.

Franklin visited Warm Springs with Eleanor and his secretary, Marguerite LeHand, in the autumn of 1924. When he took his first dip in the resort's pool, a "heavenly warmth" flowed over his legs. "How marvelous it feels," he said. "I don't think I'll ever get out!"

From then on, he spent several hours a day in the pool. Soon he was able to move his right leg for the first time in three years, and he began to hope for a miracle. "If I could only drop my business and stay here for a whole year, I am convinced that I would be able to get around without crutches," he told a friend.

He was so taken with Warm Springs that he purchased the resort in 1926. At the time, the place consisted of a dilapidated old hotel, fifteen whitewashed cottages, the mineral-water pool, and twelve hundred acres of surrounding woodland. Roosevelt set about rebuilding the resort, converting it into an international center for the study and treatment of infantile paralysis. In 1927, he formed the nonprofit Georgia Warm Springs Foundation. Polio victims, many of them children, came to the center from all over the world.

Swimming at Warm Springs, Georgia.

For Roosevelt, Warm Springs became a second home. He had a cottage built for his own use. And he developed close ties with the surrounding community. He would spend part of each day driving down country roads and visiting outlying farms and towns in a small Ford car that had been specially rigged so he could control it entirely by hand.

By now, Roosevelt was an expert on his disease. Working with the resident physician at Warm Springs and with a growing professional staff, he developed special games and exercises, worked out charts to measure muscle growth and strength, and led his fellow "polios" in energetic games like water polo.

They called him "Dr. Roosevelt." "You've got to *know* you're going to improve," he would tell them. "Keep yourselves mentally alert. Don't lose contact with the things you enjoyed before infantile paralysis."

Roosevelt did not find a cure for polio at Warm Springs. In his own case, there was no dramatic improvement. No miracles occurred there – except, perhaps, the miracle of "Dr. Roosevelt" himself. He had renewed contact with the things he once enjoyed – with a stronger and warmer heart.

Mr. Reuben Appel of Hyde Park speaks with Governor Franklin D. Roosevelt.

TO THE WHITE HOUSE

"I pledge you, I pledge myself, to a new deal for the American people."

FRANKLIN D. ROOSEVELT

When the Democrats met for their national convention in 1928, Roosevelt was asked to make another nominating speech for Al Smith. This time, Smith won the approval of the delegates. He became the first Roman Catholic to be nominated for president by a major American political party.

Smith had been a popular New York governor, yet he knew that his chances of winning the presidency were slim. Many Americans in 1928 would not think of voting for a Catholic to be president. They feared that a Catholic might take orders from his religious leader, the pope.

Smith was also a "city boy" – a flashy dresser with a rasping New York accent – at a time when rural and small-town America was deeply suspicious of the big industrial cities with their teeming immigrant populations.

Finally, Smith was a "wet" – someone who wanted to repeal the Eighteenth Amendment to the Constitution, which prohibited the manufacture and sale of alcoholic beverages. Much of rural America was ardently "dry," opposing the repeal of the Prohibition laws.

The Republican candidate that year was Herbert Hoover, a Protestant from a small town in Iowa, and a "dry." Hoover had another advantage. During the prosperous 1920s, he had served as secretary of commerce in the administrations of Warren Harding, who died in office, and his successor, Calvin Coolidge. Hoover promised that prosperity would continue. "We in America today," he said, "are nearer to the final triumph over poverty than ever before in the history of our land."

Smith's chance for victory depended on a huge voter turnout in the major Democratic strongholds – the big industrial states of the Northeast. In order to win, he had to carry New York State, with its forty-five electoral votes. He needed a strong candidate to run for governor of New York and help swing the state into the Democratic column. Smith asked Roosevelt to run.

Roosevelt refused. He wanted to spend the rest of the year in Warm Springs, trying to exercise strength back into his legs. He was still convinced that, through exercise, he could walk again.

Smith persisted. Down in Warm Springs, Roosevelt was swamped with letters, telegrams, and phone calls from Smith and his advisers. They insisted that without Roosevelt's name on the ticket, Smith would not be able to carry New York. "I have had a difficult time turning down the Governorship," Roosevelt told his mother.

Eleanor and Louis Howe advised Roosevelt not to run. Eleanor felt that he should concentrate on his recovery and put politics aside until later. Howe was convinced that 1928 would be a bad year for the Democrats, that Smith would lose and drag Roosevelt down with him. He wanted Roosevelt to wait until 1932, and then run for governor. By 1936, Howe argued, Roosevelt would be ready to try for the presidency.

But Smith would not take no for an answer. He continued to press his case. If Roosevelt failed to help the Democratic party now, in its hour of need, he might not be able to count on party leaders to support him in some future race. Finally, Roosevelt told his secretary, Marguerite LeHand, "Well, I've got to run for governor. There's no use in all of us getting sick about it!"

Roosevelt's health immediately became a campaign issue. Rumors spread that he was physically unable to campaign, that he could not handle the governor's job. "A governor does not have to be an acrobat," Al Smith told reporters. "We do not elect him for his ability to do a double back-flip or a handspring. The work of the Governorship is brain-work. Ninety-nine percent of it is accomplished at a desk."

Roosevelt squelched the rumors about his health by campaigning throughout the state. He met the voters in every New York county, traveling by train and automobile and averaging six speeches a day. He often spoke from the backseat of an open car, standing in his leg braces as he addressed the crowd, then unlocking the braces so he could sit down again. "It's rare good fun to be back in action," he told a friend. "I had almost forgotten the thrill of it."

As most people expected, the national election was a Republican landslide. Herbert Hoover won the most sweeping victory of any presidential candidate in the nation's history. Smith – who had been elected governor of New York four times – could not even carry his home state in 1928. He lost New York by 100,000 votes.

The race for governor, however, was so close that the winner wasn't known until the last returns came in during the early morning hours. Roosevelt won, beating his Republican opponent by just 25,000 votes out of some 4,200,000 cast. He called himself the "one half of one percent Governor."

He was sworn in on January 1, 1929, in the state assembly chamber in Albany. Exactly thirty years earlier, as a sixteen-year-old boy, Franklin had watched his cousin Theodore Roosevelt take the oath of office as governor of New York in that same room.

Left hand resting on his family's old Dutch Bible, FDR takes the oath of office as governor of New York, January 1, 1929.

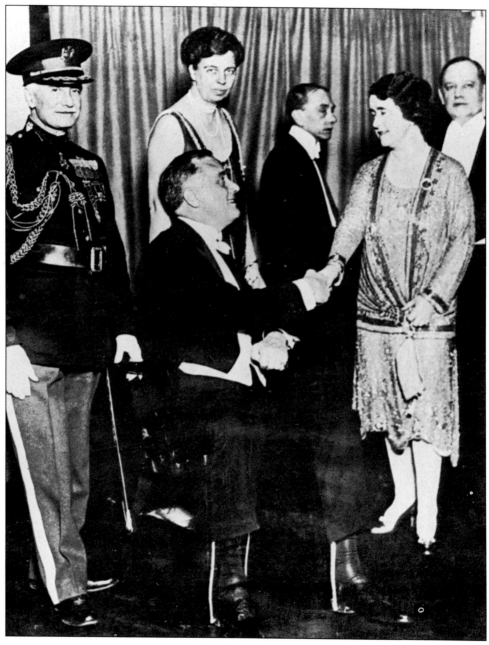

Greeting a guest at the governor's inaugural ball.

Al Smith handed over an efficient and progressive state government. Roosevelt was generous in his praise of Smith, but he wanted to establish a reputation of his own. "You know, I didn't feel able to make this campaign for governor, but I made it," he told Frances Perkins. "I didn't feel that I was sufficiently recovered to undertake the duties of Governor of New York, but here I am. . . . I've *got* to be Governor of the State of New York and I have got to be it MYSELF. If I weren't, and if I didn't do it myself, something would be wrong."

Like other progressives of that era, Roosevelt believed in using the powers of government to bring about social and economic reforms. He became the first governor of any state to favor unemployment insurance for workers who lost their jobs. He wanted New York to develop its own hydroelectric power resources, so the state could supply cheap electricity to farms, factories, and homes. He demanded adequate pensions for the elderly and improved workers' compensation laws to protect people who were injured on the job. And he asked the legislature to spend more money on schools, hospitals, and parks.

To gain public support for his programs, Roosevelt turned to a powerful new force in American life – the radio. The first commercial radio stations had appeared during the 1920s. By the time Roosevelt became governor, millions of homes had radio sets. In a series of radio reports to the citizens of New York, he explained his proposals in plain, everyday language. He persuaded thousands of listeners to send letters and telegrams to the lawmakers who opposed him.

Despite strong Republican opposition, he managed to enact much of his legislative program. And he was popular with the voters. In 1930, he won reelection to a second two-year term by a record margin – 750,001 votes. "I cast that one vote!" he told everyone.

People who saw Roosevelt on the job felt that he was having a wonderful time. He loved to joke with reporters, to hold long brainstorming sessions with his aides, to greet the endless stream of visitors to his office. He even seemed to enjoy his battles with the state legislature. "I am in one continuous glorious fight with the Republican legislative leaders," he wrote to a friend.

His informal style carried over to the ornate executive mansion in Albany. All sorts of people – officials, politicians, relatives, friends, reporters, secretaries, state troopers – were constantly coming and going. On school holidays, Roosevelt's four sons brought their friends home from Groton and Harvard. Anna, who was now married, left her baby and her German shepherd at the executive mansion when she traveled with her husband.

Eleanor tried to spend half the week in Albany, but this wasn't always possible. She was no longer the shy young woman who had politely poured tea for her husband's friends. She spent three days a week in New York City, teaching at a girls' school she had helped organize. Meanwhile, she had become increasingly active in the women's trade union movement and in Democratic politics.

Eleanor had friends and interests of her own, but her influence on her husband now was greater than ever. At his wife's urging, Roosevelt had appointed Frances Perkins as the state industrial commissioner, though he was warned that male employees would not take orders from a woman. Eleanor often gave her husband books to read, and if he seemed interested, she invited the authors to dinner. And when Franklin ran for reelection in 1930, Eleanor campaigned by his side.

Often she acted as Franklin's "eyes and ears" in places where he could not go himself. When Roosevelt inspected a state hospital, for example, he would be driven around the grounds, but it was hard for him to enter and tour the buildings. Eleanor would go in for him and report on the conditions she found. She quickly learned what to look for.

"I would tell him what was on the menu for the day," she recalled,

Governor and Mrs. Roosevelt in the back seat of their official touring car during an inspection trip to Fort Ontario, New York, July 1929.

"and he would ask: 'Did you look to see if the inmates were actually getting that food?' I learned to look into the cooking pots on the stove and to find out if the contents corresponded to the menu; I learned to notice whether the beds were too close together and whether they were folded up and put in closets behind doors during the day, which would indicate that they filled the corridors at night."

When Roosevelt took his oath as governor on New Year's Day, 1929, the United States was enjoying one of the longest economic booms in its history. Not everyone shared in the prosperity of the 1920s, but for large numbers of Americans it was the best of times in the richest land on earth.

Factories were running at full capacity. Easy credit made it possible to buy anything on the installment plan. The stock market was at an all-time high. Investors from every walk of life borrowed money to buy shares of stock in American industry, confident of making big profits.

Then it happened. On October 24, 1929 – a date remembered today as "Black Thursday" – prices on the New York Stock Exchange took an alarming nosedive. Five days later, the stock market collapsed. Panic swept through Wall Street as stockholders tried to sell their shares for whatever they would bring. Millions of shares could not be sold at all. They were worthless. Many investors who had borrowed heavily to buy stocks were wiped out during the worst day in Wall Street's history.

Exactly what set off this sudden wave of selling is still being debated today. One problem was that millions of small farmers and unskilled workers did not earn enough money during the 1920s to buy the goods pouring out of American factories. For a while, they bought on credit, but later they stopped buying altogether. As unsold goods piled up, businesses had to slow down production and the economy began to falter.

Another problem was an unsound and unregulated financial and banking system built on feverish speculation. As the stock market soared, the prices of stocks were no longer anchored to the real worth of a company. Finally, the shaky system collapsed like a house of cards.

Overnight, all confidence seemed to vanish. Investors were afraid to risk more money in business and industry. Nervous consumers cut back on their spending. Factories slowed down production and laid off workers. Without wages, the workers could not buy the products the factories produced, or even pay their bills. The biggest corporations in the country saw their markets and their business steadily shrinking.

President Hoover declared that the crisis soon would be over. But the downward cycle continued, leading to closed factories, bankrupt shops, and growing numbers of unemployed as America sank slowly into the Great Depression.

By 1930, four million Americans who wanted work could not find it. By 1931, six million people were unemployed and industrial production had dropped by half. By 1932, twelve million men and women were out of work. At the time, the United States was the only industrialized country in the world without some form of unemployment insurance or social security. In hard times, people had to depend on relatives or private charities.

In America's great cities, war veterans with medals pinned to their coats sold apples on street corners for five cents apiece. Breadlines for the hungry stretched block after block, and charity soup kitchens handed out thin porridge and weak coffee. A growing population of the homeless poor camped out in empty lots and public parks, sleeping in tents, abandoned automobiles, and makeshift shanties.

Farm prices had dropped so low that farmers couldn't afford to harvest their crops and bring them to market. Farm produce rotted in the fields while people went hungry in the cities. In Chicago, a reporter saw a crowd of fifty men, women, and children fighting over a barrel of garbage outside a restaurant.

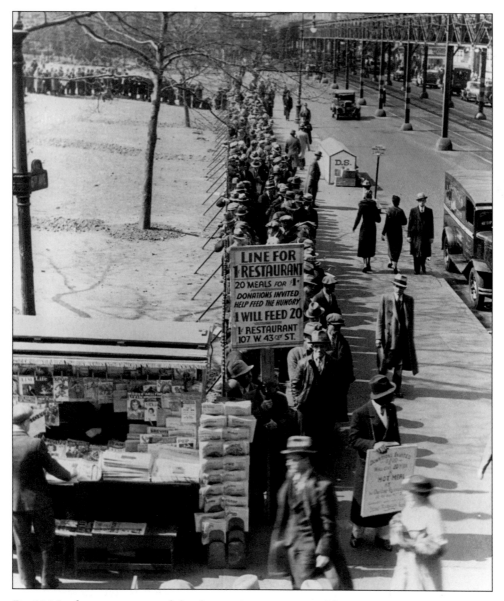

By 1932, the worst year of the depression, one out of four Americans belonged to a family that had no full-time breadwinner. This photo, taken in February 1932, shows people waiting in line for a "1¢ Restaurant" at Sixth Avenue and Forty-second Street in New York City.

Unemployed. A jobless worker on Howard Street, San Francisco's skid row.

A destitute family in the Ozark Mountains of Arkansas.

President Hoover and his advisers tried to stop the depression by propping up banks and other institutions with government loans. The banks in turn would lend the money to businesses and industries, which could then put their employees back to work. Prosperity would "trickle down" from the banks and corporations at the top of the economic ladder to the great mass of farmers and workers at the bottom.

Hoover was not willing to commit the federal government to a large-scale relief program for the unemployed. Relief was the task of local governments and private charities, he said. If Washington provided relief payments, it would undermine the self-reliance of the American people and "strike at the roots of self-government." Instead of waiting for aid from Washington, Hoover declared, people should join together in private organizations to help themselves.

Hoover's critics charged that the president was not doing enough to end the suffering and despair that seemed to get worse with each passing day. His supporters argued that the depression had to run its natural course. The economic system, through the laws of supply and demand, would eventually correct itself.

But at the height of the depression, millions of discouraged and desperate Americans were not willing to wait for the economic system to correct itself. They felt that the government should be doing something to help them. People who could not find a job, pay their rent, or feed their children wanted action. Many Americans failed to understand how the president could hand out millions of dollars in aid to banks, insurance companies, and railroads, yet insist that aid to the unemployed would destroy American individualism. They felt that the White House was shrouded in pessimism and gloom.

When the depression first began, Roosevelt agreed with Hoover that the economy would correct itself. He expected the depression to end quickly. But as things grew worse instead of better, Roosevelt's views

Homeless men huddle by a makeshift shack in a New York City vacant lot. Note the Christmas tree to the left of the shack.

changed. "New and untried remedies must at least be experimented with," he declared. And as governor of a major industrial state, he was in a position to put some of his ideas into action.

Roosevelt did not share Hoover's view that government aid to the unemployed was a threat to American values. If Washington was unwilling to act, he said, then it was up to each state to provide help for people who could not find jobs. "To those unfortunate citizens," he said, "aid must be extended by government – not as a matter of charity but as a matter of social duty."

Roosevelt's own experience had taught him that the stern doctrine of self-reliance had limitations. He himself had to depend on helping hands for such simple tasks as getting dressed or getting out of a car. A man who could not stand up by himself knew that self-reliance can carry you only so far.

Under Roosevelt's leadership, New York State set up a Temporary Emergency Relief Administration (TERA). "It is clear to me," he said, "that it is the duty of those who have benefited by our industrial and economic system to come to the front in such a grave emergency and assist in relieving those who under the same system are the losers and sufferers." TERA's first priority was to provide jobs for the unemployed. People were put to work on a variety of public works, soil conservation, and reforestation projects. When work could not be found, the agency provided food, clothing, and shelter to the needy. By 1932, TERA was providing some form of relief for nearly one family out of ten in New York State.

New York became the first state in the nation to fight unemployment by direct government action. To do this, Roosevelt had to double the state income tax. His critics charged that he would bankrupt New York. His admirers regarded him as the governor who had done the most to relieve suffering and put people back to work. And as the presidential election of 1932 approached, Roosevelt emerged as a leading candidate.

Presidential candidates had often called on industrialists and financiers for advice. Roosevelt recruited a group of brilliant young professors from Columbia University. Representing a variety of viewpoints and opinions, they became known as his "brain trust."

Members of the brain trust would take a late afternoon train to Albany, have dinner with Roosevelt, then gather round the fireplace in the governor's study. He would bring up a problem he wanted to discuss.

Then, as brain truster Raymond Moley recalled, "We were off at an exciting and exhausting clip. . . . He would listen with rapt attention for a few minutes and then break in with a question. . . . Those darting questions of Roosevelt's were the ticks of the evening's metronome. The intervals between them would grow shorter. The questions themselves would become meatier, more informed. . . . By midnight . . . the Governor, scorning further questions, would be making vigorous pronouncements on the subject we had been discussing, waving his cigarette holder to emphasize his points."

One result of those brainstorming sessions was an attack on Hoover's "trickle-down" economic policies. In a nationwide radio address, Roosevelt declared that the government must not only lend money at the top, to banks and corporations, but must also protect small businessmen, farmers, and homeowners. He called for government programs "that build from the bottom up and not from the top down, that put their faith once more in the forgotten man at the bottom of the economic pyramid." The phrase "forgotten man" touched a nerve among millions of ordinary people who had been hard hit by the depression. They felt that Roosevelt understood their plight and would do something about it.

Roosevelt turned to professors for advice, but for the day-to-day operations of his political campaign, he relied on a staff of tough political pros. His longtime aide, the gaunt and excitable Louis Howe, was in charge of Roosevelt's campaign headquarters. Howe was a master of political strategy, a ghostly-looking gnome who preferred to stay behind the scenes. He worked closely with James A. Farley, a big, cheerful man with a genial manner and a phenomenal memory for names and faces. Farley traveled around the country, lining up support for Roosevelt.

The Democrats held their convention in Chicago that year. Roosevelt stayed in Albany, in constant touch with Farley and Howe by telephone, listening to the convention speeches on the radio. He won the presidential nomination on the fourth ballot.

*FDR with his top aides, Louis Howe (left) and Jim Farley, during the 1932
presidential campaign.*

By custom, the nominee always waited for a committee to visit him
and inform him officially of the convention's choice. Roosevelt decided to
break that tradition. Here was his chance to show the nation that he
could move swiftly and act decisively. He would make a dramatic gesture
that looked to the future rather than the past. At a time when commercial
air travel was still an adventure, he would fly to Chicago and accept the
nomination in person.

With Eleanor, two of his sons, three secretaries, two bodyguards, and
his speechwriter, Samuel I. Rosenman, Roosevelt boarded a chartered

plane in Albany. Flying against strong headwinds, the little Ford Tri-
motor bounced through the sky as Roosevelt and Rosenman sat in the
cold, noisy cabin working on the governor's acceptance speech. After re-
fueling stops in Buffalo and Cleveland, they touched down at Chicago
nine hours after leaving Albany. It was the first time that a presidential
candidate had made a campaign trip by plane.

From the airport, Roosevelt was driven directly to Chicago Stadium to
address the convention. "I pledge you, I pledge myself, to a new deal for
the American people," he told the wildly cheering crowd of delegates and
spectators. "This is more than a political campaign; it is a call to arms.
Give me your help, not to win votes alone, but to win in this crusade to
restore America to its greatness."

*Arriving in Chicago by air to accept his party's nomination for president, FDR
is swamped by reporters and photographers.*

"This is more than a political campaign; it is a call to arms!" FDR addresses the Democratic National Convention in Chicago, July 2, 1932.

The term "New Deal," almost hidden in his speech, quickly caught on. It became the watchword of Roosevelt's political program.

The campaign of 1932 took place during the darkest days of the depression. Fairly or not, Hoover had become a symbol of the depression in the minds of millions of Americans. A moon-faced man who seldom smiled, he seemed stiff and uncomfortable in the public eye. Many people held him personally responsible for their misfortunes. When his campaign train pulled into Detroit, mounted police had to break up an angry mob shouting, "Hang him! Hang him!"

Compared with the unsmiling president, Roosevelt seemed to radiate optimism. To show the public he was physically fit, he set off on a strenuous campaign, traveling across the country and speaking from the rear

Campaigning in Indianapolis, Indiana, October 20, 1932.

platform of his train, "the Roosevelt Special." There was only one campaign issue – the depression. Roosevelt assailed Hoover's policies. While he called for direct government action, he did not spell out a clear program of his own. But if his speeches were vague, they always expressed confidence and faith in the future.

The outcome of the election was never in doubt. Roosevelt defeated Hoover by more than seven million votes and carried forty-two of the forty-eight states. The Democrats won big majorities in both houses of Congress.

After Hoover had conceded on election night, Roosevelt went from his campaign headquarters to his New York City townhouse, where his mother embraced him at the door. "This is the greatest night of my life!" he said. Later, his son James helped him into bed.

James bent over to kiss his father good night. Roosevelt looked up at him and said, "You know, Jimmy, all my life I have been afraid of only one thing – fire. Tonight I think I'm afraid of something else."

"Afraid of what, Pa?"

"I'm afraid that I may not have the strength to do this job."

Then he asked Jimmy to pray for him.

FDR shares the rear platform of his 1932 campaign train with vice-presidential candidate John Nance Garner.

SIX

FDR AND THE GREAT DEPRESSION

*"The admirable trait in Roosevelt is that
he has the guts to try."*

SENATOR HIRAM JOHNSON

While Roosevelt waited to take office, the depression grew worse by the
day. Four months would pass between his election in November and his
inauguration the following March. During that gloomy winter, the country was gripped by uncertainty and fear.

Across the land, factories lay idle and farmers burned crops they could
not sell. As much as a third of the nation's work force was unemployed.
No one knew exactly how many people were out of work.

Uneasy about the future, bank depositors stood in long lines, waiting
to withdraw their savings. Since a bank uses most of the money it takes
in to make loans, many institutions did not have enough cash on hand to
meet the massive demand for withdrawals. Thousands of banks failed,
taking the savings of small depositors with them.

By inauguration day – March 4, 1933 – every state in the Union had
ordered its remaining banks to close. The stock and grain markets had
shut down. The U.S. Treasury did not have enough currency to meet the

government payroll. The economy of the world's richest country was at a standstill, waiting to hear what the new president intended to do.

On that raw Saturday afternoon under overcast skies, Franklin Delano Roosevelt stood in his steel braces before Charles Evans Hughes, chief justice of the Supreme Court. Placing his hand on the family Bible that had recorded Roosevelt births and deaths for 263 years, he took his oath as the thirty-second president of the United States. Then he turned to face the expectant crowd of one hundred thousand in front of the Capitol building. Standing bareheaded as the biting wind ruffled his gray hair, Roosevelt gripped the sides of the metal speaker's stand. His voice rang with great self-confidence as he called on Americans to renew their faith in themselves and their system of government:

"This is preeminently a time to speak the truth, the whole truth, frankly and boldly. Nor need we shrink from honestly facing conditions in our country today. This great nation will endure as it has endured, will revive and will prosper. So first of all let me assert my firm belief that the only thing we have to fear is fear itself. . . ."

The most urgent task, he declared, was to put people back to work. Speaking like a general rallying his troops, Roosevelt pledged immediate action to combat the depression: "This nation asks for action, and action now. . . . I shall ask Congress for . . . broad Executive power to wage a war against the emergency, as great as the power that would be given to me if we were in fact invaded by a foreign foe."

It was the first inaugural address to be broadcast widely on the radio. The new president's words crackled over the airwaves to millions of listeners, delivering a message of courage and hope that Americans had been waiting to hear.

Roosevelt had promised "action and action now." He moved with breathtaking speed to meet the emergency and restore confidence.

First he declared a four-day "bank holiday." When Americans woke

Inauguration Day, March 4, 1933. Chief Justice Charles Evans Hughes administers the oath of office. To the right of FDR are his son James and (with head bowed) the outgoing president, Herbert Hoover. At far left, wearing a hat and carrying a bouquet, stands Eleanor Roosevelt. FDR was the last president to wait four months between his election in November and his inauguration. Under the Twentieth Amendment to the Constitution, Inauguration Day was moved up to January 20, beginning in 1936.

up Monday morning, they learned that the federal government had shut down every bank in the country. The only money they could lay their hands on was in their pockets and purses.

Next, Roosevelt summoned Congress into a special session. Meeting in Washington five days after the inauguration, the lawmakers quickly passed the Emergency Banking Relief Act. This law gave the new president sweeping powers to deal with the nation's shaky banking system. Every bank would be examined. Only the stronger banks would be allowed to reopen. The others would be administered by federal "conservators" until their future could be decided.

There was little opposition to the new law. "The house is burning down," said a Republican congressman, "and the President of the United States says this is the way to put out the fire."

President Roosevelt and members of his cabinet pose for the first photograph taken in FDR's White House office. Frances Perkins (back row, far right) was the first woman ever chosen to serve in a president's cabinet.

During his first week in office, Roosevelt also introduced two regular features of his administration – open press conferences and "fireside chats" by radio to the American people. At his first press conference, 125 reporters crowded around the president's desk in the oval office. They were happy to hear that they no longer had to submit written questions in advance – as required by presidents Hoover, Coolidge, and Harding. Instead, Roosevelt was willing to meet the reporters on their own ground. Questions could be fired at him on the spot.

Reporters crowd around the president's desk at his first White House press conference on March 8, 1933. During his twelve years in office, FDR held 998 press conferences.

"He was thoroughly at ease," said one reporter. "He made no effort to conceal his pleasure in the give and take of the situation." When the conference ended, the reporters did something they had never done before. They gave the man they were covering a spontaneous round of applause.

Roosevelt's first fireside chat was broadcast to a radio audience of sixty million. "My friends," the president said, "I want to talk for a few minutes with the people of the United States about banking. . . . I want to tell you what has been done in the last few days, why it was done, and what the next steps are going to be."

He presented his case in simple terms and urged people to return their savings to the bank. "It is safer to keep your money in a reopened bank than it is under the mattress," he promised. The next morning, people lined up to put their money back into the bank instead of taking it out. Within a week, three out of every four banks were open for business.

Letters and telegrams poured into the White House, praising the president for his decisive acts. As the nation responded to a new sense of leadership, fear and uncertainty gave way to optimism and hope. "The admirable trait in Roosevelt is that he has the guts to try," said Hiram Johnson, the Republican senator from California. "He does it all with the rarest good nature. . . . We have exchanged for a frown in the White House a smile. Where there were hesitation and vacillation . . . feebleness, timidity, and duplicity, there are now courage and boldness and real action."

With Congress and the public firmly behind him, Roosevelt had set the stage for a whirlwind of legislative accomplishment that would change the character of American life. The lawmakers stood ready to do practically anything the president asked. Bills originating in the White House and sent to Capitol Hill were passed almost daily. This hectic period became known as the "Hundred Days." In that time, Congress passed more legislation than in any previous session in history.

*A newspaper cartoon pokes fun at the New Deal's numerous alphabetical
agencies.*

A small army of bright young men and women — lawyers, economists,
social workers, professors — had descended on Washington to take up
arms against the depression and help shape the New Deal. Lights burned
late in government offices all over town as they drafted bills and regula-
tions and set up dozens of new agencies. Roosevelt was admired for his
ability to find outstanding talent and inspire devotion in those who
worked for him. "He is the best picker of brains I ever saw," said an aide.

As the New Deal took form, its programs and policies often seemed haphazard and chaotic. Critics charged that the president was plunging ahead recklessly without knowing where he was going. Yet Roosevelt had three tasks clearly in mind. They were called the "three R's" — relief, recovery, and reform. In fact, the New Deal seemed to be carrying on a romance with the alphabet as it spawned a bewildering array of government programs and agencies from the AAA to the WPA. Roosevelt himself became known by his initials — FDR.

FDR visits a Civilian Conservation Corps camp in Virginia's Shenandoah Valley, August 12, 1933.

The first priority was to provide relief for the destitute and unemployed. Some New Deal relief programs were intended to feed the hungry and assist the needy with money. But most of them were designed to create useful jobs.

One of the earliest and most popular of these programs was the Civilian Conservation Corps – the CCC. This agency hired unemployed young men between the ages of seventeen and twenty-eight and put them to work in national forests and parks – planting trees, fighting fires, building ranger stations and lookout towers, improving beaches and campgrounds. Hundreds of recreation areas and wildlife refuges in use today were created by the CCC.

Members of the corps lived in camps run by the army. They earned a dollar a day plus room, board, and clothing. Altogether, 2½ million young men served in the CCC between 1933 and 1942, when the corps was disbanded because of World War II. Tens of thousands were taught to read and write in the CCC, and thousands went on to college.

Another agency, the National Youth Administration (NYA), helped two million depression-squeezed young people complete their educations. Under this program, high school and college students were paid to work part-time in libraries and as research assistants. Without aid from the NYA, many of them would have dropped out of school.

Of all the New Deal agencies created to provide jobs, the biggest and most visible was the Works Progress Administration (WPA). WPA workers built roads, airports, post offices, hospitals, playgrounds, and schools from Maine to California. They taught adult education courses, served hot lunches to schoolchildren, and set up medical and dental clinics. They translated millions of pages into Braille, recorded hundreds of traditional folk tunes, spirituals, and American Indian songs, and interviewed more than two thousand surviving ex-slaves to make a permanent record of their experiences.

A WPA work crew repairs a flood-damaged street in Louisville, Kentucky.

Georgia's first WPA Bookmobile. It gave employment to one WPA and two NYA workers and distributed books throughout Thomas County.

Special WPA projects gave unemployed artists, writers, and musicians a chance to practice their crafts. "After all," said FDR, "they have to eat too." WPA artists painted murals on the walls of post offices, schools, and federal buildings. Writers turned out a variety of nonfiction books, including a highly regarded series of guides to every state and territory. Actors, singers, and musicians brought plays and concerts to millions of people who had never seen a live performance.

Like most New Deal programs, the WPA came in for plenty of criticism. A new word was coined — *boondoggling* — to describe the agency's make-work projects as a waste of money. But during the decade in which it functioned, the WPA provided work for eight million people, took advantage of their special skills, and helped change the face of America. The agency's director, Harry L. Hopkins, was guided by his conviction that it was better to create productive jobs than to simply hand out relief payments.

Along with unemployment relief on a massive scale, New Deal planners came up with elaborate programs for economic recovery. To help rescue the nation's farmers, Congress created the Agricultural Adjustment Administration (AAA). Farmers had long received low prices for their crops because they grew more food than the country could use. The goal of the AAA was to raise farm prices by reducing the nation's huge food surpluses — an idea that has influenced farm policy ever since. Under this program, farmers were paid government subsidies to limit the size of basic crops. By 1935, more than thirty million acres had been taken out of production. Farm prices had soared, rising 50 percent.

Many farmers praised the Triple A, but others complained that the benefits went mainly to big landowners. Consumers complained about higher food prices. Some critics denounced the AAA for trying to end want in the midst of plenty by doing away with plenty. While poor people went hungry, farmers plowed under crops and let land stand idle.

What the AAA was to farmers, the NRA was to the business community. The National Recovery Administration allowed each industry to draw up "codes of fair competition," which regulated production, prices, and working conditions. This program guaranteed workers the right to organize and join labor unions. And it established the principle of maximum hours of labor and minimum wages on a national basis for the first time.

FDR had great hopes for the NRA, but it quickly ran into trouble. With some 750 industry codes to enforce, the agency became a cumbersome bureaucracy. Small businessmen charged that the codes favored big corporations and encouraged monopoly. Labor leaders complained that the NRA was biased in favor of employers, and that it offered unions little protection. Strikers on a Baltimore picket line carried signs that read NRA Means National Run Around.

In addition to measures for relief and recovery, the New Deal introduced basic reforms that have become enduring features of American life. The Federal Deposit Insurance Corporation (FDIC) was created to insure bank deposits. When a bank fails today, depositors are protected by the FDIC. They do not lose their life's savings. The Security and Exchange Commission (SEC) was set up to regulate the stock market. It still protects investors from abuses that contributed to the stock market crash of 1929.

Another lasting New Deal reform was Social Security. When Roosevelt took office in 1933, old-age assistance and unemployment insurance were already common in Europe and in industrial nations like Canada and Australia. The United States began to catch up in 1935 when Congress passed the Social Security Act. Under this program, the federal government used employer and employee contributions to make pension payments to the aged and the disabled. The act also provided unemployment insurance for workers who lost their jobs, so they could collect payments while looking for new work.

At first, only about half of all workers were eligible for unemployment insurance, and benefits paid to the aged and disabled were small. Even so, the Social Security Act aroused bitter opposition. It was attacked as being too expensive, as "socialistic," and as a violation of the traditional values of thrift and self-help. And yet Social Security was so popular that the opposition faded away.

The first social security numbers were issued to American workers in 1935.

"Today a hope of many years' standing is fulfilled," said FDR on signing the bill. "We have tried to frame a law which will give some measure of protection to the average citizen and his family against the loss of a job and against a poverty-ridden old age."

The Wagner Act, also passed in 1935, was hailed by union leaders as a bill of rights for labor. This law strengthened earlier labor legislation. It set up the National Labor Relations Board (NLRB), which continues to function today. The NLRB conducted elections when workers wanted to choose a union to represent them. And it prohibited employers from interfering with union organizing activities.

Of all the New Deal projects, the most spectacular was the Tennessee Valley Authority (TVA). This vast social experiment reflected FDR's long-standing interest in conservation and public power. The goal of the TVA was to reclaim the impoverished Tennessee Valley basin, an area of

640,000 square miles winding through seven southern states. Floods regularly devastated the valley. Ninety-seven percent of the farms had no electricity. Malaria and tuberculosis were rampant, and a million families lived on cornmeal and salt pork.

In time, the TVA built a series of dams and hydroelectric projects to control floods and supply electric power to the valley's farms, factories, and homes. Critics charged that the mammoth government project was a reckless adventure in socialism. Yet the TVA was welcomed by the people it served. It brought both electricity and better times to one of the poorest regions of the country and served as a model of government planning for nations around the world.

During his first term, FDR put together the most ambitious legislative program in the nation's history. So many things were going on at once that it was hard to keep track of them. And while the New Deal had not conquered the depression, the crisis had passed. By 1936, the country seemed to be on the road to recovery.

Millions of new jobs had been created. Industrial production was increasing, and corporate profits were the highest since the crash of 1929. Payrolls had doubled. The cash income of farmers had almost doubled. Special government loan programs had saved thousands of homes and farms from foreclosure.

As the 1936 presidential election approached, Roosevelt was at the height of his popularity. Many Americans regarded him as their personal hero. They thought of him as a president who was concerned with their welfare, and of his government as a caring one.

Still, criticism persisted. Roosevelt's opponents charged that FDR and the radicals around him were strangling free enterprise and turning the country into a welfare state. The president's critics denounced government interference with business. They argued that the New Deal had given too much power to labor unions. And they condemned the growing national debt (thirty-six billion dollars by 1936) that had resulted from the government's emergency relief programs.

To help pay for these programs, Congress had passed a new tax bill in 1935, sharply raising taxes for big corporations and wealthy individuals. Opposition newspapers branded the tax bill the "Soak the Successful Act." They called the New Deal the "Raw Deal."

Increased taxes aroused bitter resentment. Never before had Roosevelt been the target of such intensely personal attacks. To FDR haters – and there were plenty of them – he was a "traitor to his class," a dangerous man intoxicated by power. At a country club in Connecticut, members were forbidden to mention Roosevelt's name. There was even a whispering campaign that he was insane.

Opposition reached into the ranks of the Democratic party. A group of conservative Democrats, including the one-time Happy Warrior Al Smith, organized the Liberty League, dedicated to the defeat of the New Deal. Smith attacked Roosevelt as "the destroyer of the Constitution," and a reckless spendthrift who threatened to drag the country down to ruin.

On the political Left, Roosevelt was accused of not doing enough to change the economic system that had brought misery to so many. These critics argued that he should have nationalized the banks, railroads, and public utilities during the crisis of 1933, when he had the chance. They said that FDR was trying to prop up a failed system that needed total reform.

No president since Abraham Lincoln had aroused such intense antagonism and angry debate. Roosevelt was called everything from a Communist to a Fascist. Yet he insisted that he was just trying to steer a sensible middle course. In the language of the sea, he spoke of sailing the ship of state through perilous waters, with "thunder on the left" and "thunder on the right."

FDR talks to Steve Brown, a North Dakota homesteader, during a tour of the drought-stricken Midwest in August 1936.

Roosevelt's critics charged that he had one solution for every problem—big spending—and that he would bankrupt the country.

He had no desire to change the economic system, he declared. Rather, he wanted to nurse the system back to health. And he wanted to bring about reforms that would make the system more just and humane, so that people would not suffer from poverty and neglect.

"No one in the United States believes more firmly than I do in the system of private business, private property, and private profit," Roosevelt said. "It was this administration which saved the system of private profit and free enterprise after it had been dragged to the brink of ruin."

The most damaging opposition to the New Deal came from within the government itself, from the U.S. Supreme Court. Beginning in 1935, the Court dealt a series of devastating blows to New Deal planners. First the Court ruled that the NRA – Roosevelt's program for industrial recovery

– was unconstitutional. Then the Court struck down the AAA – Roosevelt's farm program. Later, the justices went on to rule against several other pieces of New Deal legislation. They argued that the federal government had invaded the rights of the states and was interfering illegally in the nation's social and economic life.

The NRA and the AAA had been the cornerstones of FDR's program for economic recovery, and he angrily denounced the Court. He charged that the justices were insisting on too strict and narrow a view of the federal government's powers to regulate business and commerce.

The 1936 election gave Roosevelt a chance to take his case to the people. At the Democratic convention in Philadelphia, the president was renominated by acclamation. In his acceptance speech, he lashed out at the "economic royalists" and "privileged princes" who opposed his policies. "These economic royalists complain that we seek to overthrow the institutions of America," he said. "What they really complain of is that we seek to take away their power. . . . There is a mysterious cycle in human events. To some generations much is given. Of other generations much is expected. This generation of Americans has a rendezvous with destiny."

Roosevelt's Republican opponent was Alfred M. Landon, the amiable, slow-speaking governor of Kansas. Landon charged that FDR was ignoring the Constitution and creating a huge federal bureaucracy at the expense of freedom. He called the president "Franklin Deficit Roosevelt."

Roosevelt acknowledged that vast sums had been spent on relief, but only to keep people from starving. He campaigned as the champion of the "forgotten man." "There's one issue in this campaign," he said. "It's myself, and people must be either for me or against me."

Wherever he went on his nationwide campaign trip – whistle-stopping across the prairies and plains, riding in motorcades through jammed city streets – jubilant crowds were on hand to cheer and wave and reach out

FDR and Eleanor greet the crowds from the rear platform of the presidential special during the campaign of 1936.

to touch the president. Even the weather seemed to favor FDR. As his campaign train arrived in the Middle West, which was suffering from an extended drought, rain began to fall.

Almost every newspaper in the country opposed Roosevelt. But the voters were on his side. On election day, the president defeated Landon by nearly eleven million votes, the biggest popular plurality ever recorded. Roosevelt carried every state except Maine and Vermont, winning 523 electoral votes to only 8 for Landon — the most lopsided electoral victory since the election of 1820. In the new Congress, the Democrats won so many seats — outnumbering the Republicans by four to one — that some Democrats had to sit on the Republican side of the aisle.

For FDR, it was a triumphant personal victory. As Kansas editor William Allen White put it, "He has been all but crowned by the people."

Victory. On the front porch at Hyde Park, the president and members of his family acknowledge the cheers of neighbors on election night, November 3, 1936. With FDR are (left to right) his daughter Anna, his son John, his mother Sara, his son Franklin, Jr., and Eleanor.

Joking with reporters at Hyde Park, July 4, 1937.

THE MOST COMPLICATED MAN

*"He was the most complicated
human being I ever knew."*
FRANCES PERKINS

Few presidents seemed to be having as good a time as Franklin Roosevelt. No matter how tough things were, he presided over the country with a jaunty exuberance that rarely failed.

Visitors marveled at his ability to relax in the midst of crisis. Sometimes he conducted business in the White House swimming pool. A visiting dignitary might find himself splashing about with the president as FDR practiced his backstroke and kept up a barrage of questions.

"He was full of the fun of life," said Nicholas Roosevelt, the president's Republican cousin. "As I watched his handsome head over the water of the pool and listened to his genial comments, I kept saying to myself: 'It's not possible. This delightful, youthful-looking man in this pool cannot be the President of the United States.' "

Not since the days of Andrew Jackson had life in the White House been so informal and easygoing. The second-floor living quarters were cluttered with family mementoes and comfortable old furniture, some of it brought down from Hyde Park. Books and magazines were strewn about everywhere. The president's Scottish terrier, Fala, romped through the halls, greeted visitors, and slept in his master's room at night. And every morning, Roosevelt's grandchildren burst into his room to tumble about on his bed as he ate breakfast from a tray and read the newspapers.

He worked in his bedroom until 10:00 or 10:30, reviewing the day's business and going over reports. Then he was taken by elevator to his downstairs office. He used a small wheelchair without arms, so he could swing himself into the swivel chair behind his desk.

"Come on in!" he would boom out as he waved each visitor in. Genial and outgoing, he delighted in new faces and greeted everyone like an old friend.

FDR clearly liked people, and he wanted to be liked in return. With few exceptions, even those who had a grudge against Roosevelt felt agreeable toward him in his presence. When Jesse H. Jones was fired from his post as secretary of commerce, he told reporters that the president was a hypocrite lacking in character. But he added: "You just can't help liking that fellow."

Roosevelt's schedule called for visitors to be ushered in at fifteen-minute intervals, but he always fell behind because he enjoyed talking so much. Conversation was his favorite method of picking up new information. He knew how to put people at ease and get them to talk about the things they knew.

As for himself, he could hold forth on any number of subjects. He could talk to an admiral about ships, a botanist about plants, an architect about buildings. Sometimes he monopolized the conversation so much that his visitor hardly had a chance to say a word.

FDR usually had lunch at his desk with a visitor, talking between mouthfuls. One of his aides, Rex Tugwell, always tried to see the president at lunchtime. Tugwell would eat his own lunch before arriving at

FDR with his secretaries: (left to right) Grace Tully, Marvin McIntyre, and Marguerite LeHand. Note the many keepsakes and mementoes that clutter the president's White House desk.

the White House. Then he would make his points while the president's mouth was full.

Talking was part of FDR's political style. By telling a long, rambling story while a visitor sat there listening, he could buy time while he was trying to make up his mind and reach a decision. If he didn't want to commit himself, he would just keep on talking until it was time for the visitor to leave. Then, with a smile and a handshake, he would say good-bye without having agreed to anything.

Roosevelt hated to say no. Visitors sometimes left his office thinking he had agreed to their proposals, when in fact he hadn't. His habit of nodding his head and murmuring "yes, yes" simply meant that he was following the conversation, not that he was agreeing. But some people misunderstood and accused him of being shifty and deceptive. His enemies said that he was two-faced. Even his friends felt that he was not always forthright, that he kept too many secrets to himself.

"You are a wonderful person, but you are one of the most difficult men to work with I have ever seen," said Harold L. Ickes, Roosevelt's secretary of the interior.

"Because I get too hard at times?" asked the president.

"No, you never get too hard. But you won't talk frankly even with people who are loyal to you and of whose loyalty you are fully convinced. You keep your cards close up against your belly."

FDR had a whole bagful of tricks up his sleeve. He would assign the same task to several people without telling any of them. As they reported back to him, one by one, he would listen sympathetically to their different points of view. Then he would make up his mind about which course to follow.

Sometimes, in order to win support for a policy he favored, FDR would deliberately adopt the opposite point of view. Then he would allow himself to be talked out of it. After he took office in 1933, he told Democratic Senator Tom Connolly that emergency relief measures would have to be cut back because of a limited budget and constitutional restrictions on the president's power. Connolly was horrified. "If it was constitutional to spend forty billion dollars in a war [World War I]," the senator said, "isn't it just as constitutional to spend a little money to relieve the hunger and misery of our citizens?"

That's just what Roosevelt wanted to hear. He didn't say a word as Connolly argued eloquently for massive relief measures — the same policy that Roosevelt had secretly favored all along.

Those who knew FDR were fascinated by the mysteries and contradictions of his personality. He could ask Congress to appropriate billions, yet he himself would work patiently on a knot in order to save the string. He delighted in new faces, new ideas, and new projects, but in his personal habits he resisted change, wearing favorite old sweaters with holes in them and living all his life in the house where he was born.

With his quick smile and easy charm, he seemed the most open of men. And yet those closest to him felt that they did not really know him at all. William Phillips, an old friend, said that FDR had "at least three or four different personalities. He could turn from one personality to another with such speed that you never knew where you were or to which personality you were talking."

And Frances Perkins, Roosevelt's secretary of labor, commented: "That quality of simplicity which we delight to think marks the great and noble was not his. He was the most complicated human being I ever knew."

The president usually left his office around 5:30 P.M., went for a swim, then relaxed with cocktails before dinner at 9:00. He loved company, and with people he knew well, he would let his hair down and pretend to be just one of the boys. He enjoyed frequent poker games with a group of cronies, and he was thrilled when he outbluffed vice-president John Nance Garner, said to be the best poker player in Washington.

When there were no guests or social events, Roosevelt might spend the evening alone in his study, relaxing with his stamp collection or working with painstaking care on the scale models of sailing ships he had collected most of his life. Eleanor might drop in to call his attention to a book she was reading, to urge her husband to see someone or do something, or simply to sit with him and chat.

Eleanor had gone to the White House with misgivings. "I never wanted to be a president's wife," she told her close friend and confidante, the Associated Press reporter Lorena Hickock. Over the years, Eleanor had

The stamp collector. The Post Office Department presented FDR with the first sheet of each new issue, and the State Department sent him any unusual stamps that arrived in the mail. Roosevelt sometimes suggested subjects for new stamps, and he even designed some himself.

established a reputation of her own as a writer, educator, and social reformer. When Franklin became president, she feared at first that she would be confined to the traditional role of first lady as the White House hostess.

Yet Eleanor quickly became the most influential first lady the White House had ever seen. Soon she was flying all over the country, making on-the-spot investigations, reporting back to the president on what she had seen and heard, and gathering material for her syndicated newspaper column "My Day."

Eleanor and Franklin hold an informal press conference as reporters crowd around their car in Warm Springs, Georgia, November 1938.

Some administration officials resented Eleanor and accused her of meddling. "I wish that Mrs. Roosevelt would stick to her knitting and keep out of the affairs connected with my department," complained Harold Ickes. "After all, the people did not elect her President."

Yet FDR had great confidence in his wife's eyewitness reports and shrewd assessments. Sometimes he insisted on an action that local officials thought unnecessary because Mrs. Roosevelt had seen the situation with her own eyes. She had reported so vividly that he felt he too had seen. Millions of people all over the world came to admire Eleanor's energy, warmth, and compassion.

In her passionate support of equal rights for women and civil rights for blacks, Eleanor was several steps ahead of her husband and miles ahead of the country as a whole. Partly because of her, the Roosevelts entertained a great variety of people, including many who found the White House open to them for the first time. Spokesmen for minority groups, labor leaders, movie stars, writers, artists, and explorers all found themselves sitting around the same table in the White House dining room.

Eleanor urged Franklin to appoint blacks and women to responsible posts and to support laws banning discrimination. During the Roosevelt administration, women made an impact on the federal government for the first time. Along with Frances Perkins, the first woman ever chosen for a cabinet post, FDR named America's first female envoy and the first woman judge of the U.S. Court of Appeals. And he broke with the past by appointing more blacks to responsible positions than all previous presidents combined.

Roosevelt also insisted that blacks be included in significant numbers in the New Deal's relief and work programs. For the first time in the segregated South, black workers were paid the same wages as whites and were visible in supervisory jobs. But when it came to civil rights legislation, Roosevelt's record was weak. He felt he could not afford to anger powerful segregationist congressmen because he needed their support to

Royal visit. The Roosevelts greet King George and Queen Elizabeth of Great Britain at Union Station in Washington, D.C., June 8, 1939. FDR holds the arm of his aide, Brigadier General Edwin M. Watson.

push through vital New Deal programs. Even so, blacks scored major gains under the New Deal.

Franklin and Eleanor were both exceptionally strong-willed people. And while they led independent lives, they were also close. "We are really very dependent on each other though we do see so little of each other," Eleanor wrote from one of her trips. "I miss you and hate to feel you so far away. . . ."

Franklin sometimes teased his wife about her reputation as a "do-gooder," but he was enormously proud of her and would not allow anyone to criticize her in his presence. A portrait of Eleanor hung over the door of his White House study. It had been painted long before, when she was very young. Once, when Frances Perkins was leaving the president's study, she paused in front of the portrait and looked at it carefully.

"I always liked that portrait of Eleanor," FDR said. "That's just the way Eleanor looks, you know – lovely hair, pretty eyes."

Roosevelt could be warm and affectionate. Yet even with those close to him, he seldom talked about personal matters or discussed his deepest feelings. Eleanor felt there was a part of himself that her husband permitted no one to see. "He had no real confidants," she once said. "I don't think I was ever his confidante either."

And yet Roosevelt could express his feelings in deeds. His son James recalled the day the family learned that Eleanor's brother Hall had died: "Father struggled to her side and put his arm around her. 'Sit down,' he said, so tenderly. I can still hear it. And he sank down beside her and hugged her and kissed her and held her head on his chest. . . ."

With his landslide victory in 1936, Roosevelt believed that the voters had given him a mandate to push forward with his New Deal programs. Yet the Supreme Court kept blocking some of his key legislation. By January 1937, the Court had ruled against the administration in eleven of sixteen cases.

Eleanor and Franklin on the south lawn at Hyde Park.

FDR had been stung by the Court's decisions. He attacked the justices as "nine old men" (their average age was seventy-one). And he accused them of following a rigid and unreasonable interpretation of the Constitution.

Roosevelt knew, however, that age wasn't the real issue. The oldest member of the Court, eighty-one-year-old Louis Brandeis, was one of the most liberal. What galled FDR was the justices' stubborn opposition to his New Deal policies, and his own inability to influence their decisions. Supreme Court justices are appointed for life, and since FDR had taken office, none of the justices had retired or died. He was the first president in history to serve a four-year term without being able to name a single justice.

After his second inauguration, Roosevelt declared war on the Supreme Court. He asked Congress to pass a sweeping Court revision plan. For each justice who did not retire at the age of seventy, he wanted to add one new justice, up to a maximum of six. FDR claimed that the justices could not keep up with their work, that his plan was intended to improve the efficiency of the Court. But in truth, by "packing" the Court with his own appointees, he hoped to change its conservative character.

Six times before in the nation's history – including the administration of Abraham Lincoln – Congress had increased or decreased the number of justices, usually at the president's request. But the present number of nine had been fixed since 1869, and Roosevelt's court-packing plan caused an uproar. Most people felt that the president had gone too far.

In Congress, the debate over the court-packing plan was the most impassioned and divisive since the Civil War. FDR mounted a no-holds-barred campaign to pressure and persuade reluctant Democrats. And he took his case to the people, declaring in a fireside chat that the future of the New Deal was at stake.

In the end, Congress handed Roosevelt a humiliating defeat by reject-

FDR's futile attempt to "pack" the U.S. Supreme Court with six additional justices caused the biggest uproar of his peacetime presidency.

ing his Court reform plan. By that time, the Court itself had pulled the rug out from under the president by abruptly changing direction. In quick succession, the justices reversed some of their earlier opinions. And they upheld a series of New Deal measures, including the Social Security Act and the Wagner Act for labor reform. Then one of the justices retired, opening the way for Roosevelt's first appointment. After that, no important legislation was struck down by the Court. And during the next few years, Roosevelt was able to fill six more Court vacancies with his own liberal appointees.

The court-packing plan turned out to be the worst blunder of FDR's peacetime presidency. He tried to put the best face on things, claiming he had lost the battle over the Supreme Court but won the war. Yet the battle cost him a lot. For the first time, his prestige had been seriously bruised. And he had lost the support of many conservative Democrats in Congress, men who had misgivings about his New Deal policies all along. By teaming up with conservative Republicans, they were able to block much of the legislation proposed by FDR during his second term.

The New Deal had sailed into a sea of troubles. Along with the hue and cry over the Supreme Court, labor unrest had flared up across the country. The Wagner Act had given every worker the right to join a union. As workers tried to claim that right, many companies fought back, sometimes using strong-arm tactics as they tried to intimidate union organizers. Strikes, lockouts, and battles on the picket lines broke out in several major industries. Henry Ford called out his private police force to block strikers at his auto plants in Michigan. Union officials were beaten and bloodied as they tried to hand out pamphlets. The worst violence erupted on Memorial Day, 1937, at the Republic Steel plant in South Chicago, where a bloody clash between strikers and police became known as the Memorial Day Massacre.

Eventually, the unions won recognition, but the wave of strikes did nothing to bolster FDR's popularity. He had tried to remain neutral during all the labor turbulence, and he was criticized by both labor and management for not taking sides.

Meanwhile, a sharp business recession in 1937 threatened to wipe out all the gains won by the New Deal. Again, unemployment rose. Farm prices fell. Although the economy began to pick up in 1938, the Republicans scored major gains in the congressional elections that year. The Democrats still controlled Congress, but conservative opposition was strong enough to hold up most of FDR's legislative program. He finally had a Supreme Court that would approve his programs, but not a Congress that would pass them.

Labor troubles. Police subdue a picket at a strike-bound plant in Chicago, May 1937.

Commander in chief. The president with Admiral Claude C. Bloch under the big guns of the U.S.S. Houston *at San Francisco, California, July 1938.*

In his second term, Roosevelt had hoped to move rapidly toward his goals of social and economic reform. But the New Deal had lost momentum. Of course, some programs did get through Congress. The Fair Labor Standards Act, for example, established a minimum wage of twenty-five cents an hour, set a maximum work week of forty-four hours, and abolished child labor. Yet most of the president's legislative program was sidetracked by an alliance of conservative Democrats and Republicans.

A *Fortune* magazine poll taken in 1939 indicated that more than 60 percent of the American people still approved of both the president and his policies. The New Deal may have faltered, but most people did not want to see it dismantled.

Yet no New Deal program was able to conquer the depression. As late as 1939, a decade after the Wall Street crash, millions of Americans were still out of work. Unemployment would not end until World War II, when the nation's armed services and wartime industries absorbed the jobless.

Winston Churchill and FDR meet aboard the U.S.S. Augusta *in Newfoundland's Placentia Bay as the Atlantic Conference gets under way, August 1941.*

WAR CLOUDS

"Of Roosevelt . . . it must be said that had he not acted when he did, in the way he did, had he not . . . resolved to give aid to Britain, and to Europe in the supreme crisis through which we have passed, a hideous fate might well have overwhelmed mankind and made its whole future for centuries sink into shame and ruin."

WINSTON CHURCHILL

In the winter of 1933, when Franklin Roosevelt took office as president, Adolf Hitler became chancellor of Germany. Roosevelt had pledged a new deal for the American people. Hitler vowed to build the Nazi Third Reich – a German empire that would last a thousand years.

Almost single-handedly, Hitler had lifted the Nazi party from the obscurity of a Munich beer hall to control of one of Europe's mightiest nations. He made no secret of his dreams of conquest. Years before his rise to power, he had announced his plans in his book *Mein Kampf* ("My Struggle"), composed in a prison cell after an unsuccessful attempt to overthrow the German government. The leader of the Nazi party blamed Germany's defeat in World War I on betrayal by Communists and Jews. And he claimed that Germans were a "master race" destined to rule all others.

Once in power, Hitler moved swiftly to make himself absolute master of the German people. He dissolved all political parties except his own, jailed or murdered his opponents, and ruthlessly silenced any criticism in the press. Defying the Treaty of Versailles that had ended World War I, he started to rebuild the German army. "Today Germany," he declared, "to-morrow the world!"

War clouds were gathering around the globe. In Italy, the Fascist dictator Benito Mussolini had promised to start his people on the road to military glory and "national greatness." During the autumn of 1935, Italian troops invaded the helpless African kingdom of Ethiopia. In the spring of 1936, Hitler's army marched into Germany's demilitarized Rhineland district. And when civil war broke out in Spain that year, Nazi Germany and Fascist Italy both offered troops and equipment to aid the rebel forces fighting to overthrow the democratic Spanish republic.

Across the globe, Japanese military leaders were planning to establish a new order – the Greater East Asia Co-Prosperity Sphere – under Japan's political and economic domination. Japan had already occupied Korea and Manchuria. In the summer of 1937, Japanese forces launched a full-scale invasion of central China, capturing most of the country's major cities.

The dictatorships grew steadily more powerful and aggressive during the 1930s. And yet the great Western democracies – Britain, France, and the United States – stood by and did nothing at first. Weakened by the worldwide depression, the democracies were too preoccupied with their own problems to take a stand against aggression.

Few Americans admired Hitler or the Japanese warlords. Even so, they did not want to become involved in the quarrels of foreign nations. Bitter memories of World War I and dread of a future war contributed to a powerful mood of isolationism in the United States. Isolationists insisted that if war started overseas, the United States should remain neutral. War was for others, far away. Protected by wide oceans on either side, America was a fortress, safe and secure, remote from the problems of other continents.

Dictators. Italy's Benito Mussolini and Germany's Adolf Hitler.

Hitler addresses a Nazi rally in Berlin.

Early in his presidency, Roosevelt followed a hands-off policy toward events overseas. In his speeches and letters, he expressed the view that the United States should not be drawn into another foreign war. Recalling his World War I experience, he said: "I hate war. I have passed unnumbered hours, I shall pass unnumbered hours, thinking and planning how war may be kept from this nation."

An army officer bows before Japanese Emperor Hirohito.

And yet very soon, FDR came to realize that fascist bullies were a threat not only to their neighbors but to everyone on earth. In 1937, the president sounded a warning about the "reign of terror and international lawlessness" that had been unleashed upon the world. "Innocent peoples . . . innocent nations are being cruelly sacrificed to a greed for power," he said. "If those things come to pass in other parts of the world, let no one imagine that America will escape, that America may expect mercy, that this Western Hemisphere will not be attacked. . . ."

FDR compared the growth of the Axis powers (Germany, Italy, and Japan) to "an epidemic of physical disease" that threatened to spread everywhere. But he stopped short of suggesting that America abandon its neutrality. Even so, his speech caused a clamor of protest. The *Wall Street Journal* advised Roosevelt to "stop foreign meddling." Isolationist congressmen talked about impeaching the president. And a campaign was launched to get twenty-five million signatures on a petition to "Keep America Out of War."

"I am really worried about world affairs," FDR wrote a friend. "The dictator nations find their bluffs are not being called, and that encourages other nations to play the same game."

In 1938, Hitler seized control of Austria. At the Munich Conference later that year, the leaders of Great Britain and France agreed to let Germany occupy the Sudetenland, a region in western Czechoslovakia. "This is the last territorial demand I have to make in Europe," Hitler announced triumphantly. British Prime Minister Neville Chamberlain returned to London and told his people that the Munich Conference had achieved "peace with honor . . . peace in our time."

Six months later, Hitler showed his contempt for the democracies by taking over the rest of Czechoslovakia. That same month, March 1939, Fascist forces led by Francisco Franco captured Madrid, ending the civil war in Spain that had lasted three years and cost nearly a million lives.

In Germany, meanwhile, Hitler had stepped up his campaign of persecution against the Jews. On the night of November 9, 1938, Nazi storm troopers wearing civilian clothes smashed, looted, and burned Jewish shops, offices, and synagogues throughout Germany and Austria. In twenty-four hours, nearly one hundred Jews were killed and more than thirty thousand arrested and shipped off to concentration camps. So much broken glass littered the streets that the Nazi orgy of hate and destruction became known as *Kristallnacht* ("the night of the broken glass").

Roosevelt expressed shock and horror at events in Germany. "I myself could scarcely believe that such things could occur in a twentieth-century civilization," he told reporters.

Even before *Kristallnacht,* convinced that something must be done, FDR had organized an international conference to help speed the emigration of Jews and other refugees trapped in Germany. Delegates from thirty-two nations met at the French resort of Evian-les-Bains on Lake Geneva. Little was accomplished. Except for tiny Denmark and Holland, no nation was willing to let down its immigration barriers and accept large numbers of refugees. Voices were raised to condemn the Nazi crimes, but scarcely an official finger was lifted to rescue the victims of Naziism.

In the United States, isolationism was accompanied by strong feelings against further immigration. The depression was still on, and people felt there were already too many mouths to feed. Congress had refused to relax the nation's strict immigration quotas, for fear of adding to the unemployment and relief rolls. And Congress was supported by overwhelming public opinion. According to a *Fortune* magazine poll in 1938, two out of every three Americans agreed that "with conditions as they are we should try to keep [refugees] out."

Rather than fight Congress and public opinion, FDR tried to work within the existing immigration system. He set up the President's Advisory Committee on Political Refugees. He ordered the State Department to ease its restrictions so that immigration quotas from Germany and

Austria could be met in full. Against stiff opposition from both the State Department and Congress, he kept bending visa and immigration rules so that more victims of Nazi persecution could find refuge in the United States. Thousands of refugees did reach America, but thousands more were shut out.

When war broke out in Europe, the plight of the refugees grew more desperate than ever. On September 1, 1939, Hitler's troops marched into Poland. Two days later, Britain and France declared war on Germany. World War II had begun. That night, in a fireside chat, FDR told his audience: "When peace has been broken anywhere, the peace of all countries everywhere is in danger. . . . This nation will remain a neutral nation, but I cannot ask that every American remain neutral in thought as well. Even a neutral has a right to take account of facts. Even a neutral cannot be asked to close his mind or his conscience."

People everywhere were stunned by the spectacular speed of the Nazi *blitzkrieg,* or "lightning war," as German columns advanced through Poland from the west. On September 17, Russian troops invaded Poland from the east. Polish resistance was crushed. The country was partitioned between Germany and the Soviet Union.

There was no question about America's sympathies in the war. According to a Gallup poll, 82 percent of the nation hoped for a victory by the Allies (the enemies of Hitler), while only 2 percent supported Nazi Germany. And yet most Americans continued to believe that the United States should stay out of foreign wars. Isolationists formed the America First Committee, an influential organization that opposed any direct aid to Britain and France.

Roosevelt wanted to help the Allies, but his hands were tied by the Neutrality Act of 1935, which prohibited Americans from shipping arms to nations at war. Under the provisions of this act, neither France nor Britain could purchase munitions in the United States. British officials told Washington that it would be "sheer disaster" if they could not obtain

Blitzkrieg. *A German motorized detachment rides through the bombed ruins of a Polish town, September 1939.*

American war supplies. FDR urged Congress to repeal the arms embargo. "I regret that Congress passed the Neutrality Act," he said. "I regret equally that I signed it."

Quietly, the president was lining up support in Congress. In the fall of 1939 – a month after the Nazis had overrun Poland – the arms embargo provision of the Neutrality Act was finally repealed. Now the Allies could buy anything they needed in the United States, from bullets to tanks, as long as they paid cash and carried the supplies away in their own ships.

"There is a vast difference between keeping out of war and pretending that war is none of our business," Roosevelt told Congress in his State of the Union message on January 4, 1940. "We must see the effect on our own future if all the small nations of the world have their independence snatched from them. . . . It becomes clearer and clearer that the future world will be a shabby and dangerous place to live in – yes, even for Americans to live in – if it is ruled by force in the hands of a few."

In the spring of 1940, after several months of an inactive *sitzkrieg*, or "sitting war," Hitler struck again. German forces occupied Denmark and Norway in April, Holland and Belgium in May, then swept toward Paris. From London, Britain's new prime minister, Winston Churchill, sent an urgent message to Roosevelt: "The scene has darkened swiftly. . . . The small countries are simply smashed up, one by one, like matchwood. . . . We expect to be attacked here ourselves. . . ."

France surrendered on June 22, leaving Great Britain to battle the Nazi war machine alone. "The long night of barbarism," as Churchill called it, descended on Europe.

The Nazi conquest of western Europe was a shock to most Americans. They realized now that they could not live in isolation from the rest of the world. That summer, Congress appropriated money for a massive buildup of American military forces and approved the nation's first peacetime draft. Roosevelt promised all-out aid to Britain, short of war. And after months of indecision, he decided to seek a third term.

FDR looks on as a blindfolded Secretary of War, Henry L. Stimson, draws the first draft numbers in the national selective service lottery, October 29, 1940—beginning the nation's first peacetime draft.

No American president had ever served more than two terms. Long before the 1940 election, Roosevelt's intentions had become a national guessing game. Probably, the president himself wasn't sure what he would do. "I do not want to run," he told Treasury Secretary Henry Morgenthau, Jr., "unless . . . things get very, very much worse in Europe."

When German troops marched into Paris on June 14, FDR finally made up his mind. At the Democratic National Convention in Chicago that summer, he won renomination on the first ballot.

The Republicans nominated Wendell L. Willkie, a dynamic self-made businessman from Indiana and the toughest opponent Roosevelt had ever faced. Willkie hammered away at the third-term issue. It was dangerous to let one man serve as president for twelve years, he said. He warned that FDR's reelection would be "the last step in the destruction of our democracy." And as the campaign heated up, he charged that Roosevelt would lead the nation into war. "If his promise to keep our boys out of

Wendell Willkie, the Republican presidential candidate, waves his straw hat to hometown supporters in Elwood, Indiana, August 17, 1940.

foreign wars is no better than his promise to balance the budget, they're already almost on the transports," said Willkie.

Roosevelt called the charges a "deliberate falsification of fact," and he accused Willkie and the Republicans of "playing politics with national defense." He told a cheering campaign rally, "I am an old campaigner, and I love a good fight!"

As the candidates traded charges, Britain was battling for survival. Day

FDR speaks at a political rally in Newburgh, New York, November 4, 1940.

after day, squadrons of Nazi bombers roared across the English Channel to blast London and other British cities. Packs of U-boats, operating out of conquered ports on the French and Norwegian coasts, prowled the Atlantic, attacking the convoys of ships that were Britain's lifeline.

Months before the U.S. election, Winston Churchill had pleaded with Roosevelt for help. Churchill wanted fifty or sixty American destroyers. He said that the ships were vitally necessary to protect Britain's supply routes and to repel a seaborne invasion by Germany. "Mr. President," Churchill warned, "with great respect I must tell you that in the long history of the world this is a thing to do *now.*"

Facing reelection, FDR knew that Churchill's plea for destroyers posed a gigantic political risk. Isolationists argued that sending destroyers to a nation at war would itself be an act of war. Roosevelt told a friend that he might lose the election on that one issue. Even so, he decided to act quickly. "Congress is going to raise hell about this," he confided to his secretary, Grace Tully, "but even another day's delay may mean the end of civilization."

By executive order, the president arranged to transfer fifty old but usable World War I destroyers to Britain. In exchange, the United States received the right to use a string of British naval and air bases extending from Canada to the Caribbean. The trade clearly marked the end of American neutrality.

Wendell Willkie announced that he approved of the trade. But at the same time, he scolded the president for bypassing Congress. Willkie called FDR's executive order "dictatorial and arbitrary."

Two months later, when the nation's voters went to the polls, FDR still stood for leadership at a time of crisis. Roosevelt won his third term easily, defeating Willkie by nearly five million votes.

Once the election was over, the president was determined to send all possible aid to Britain. "We must become the great arsenal of democracy," he said.

The Battle of Britain, 1940. St. Paul's Cathedral stands outlined against the flames and smoke of a London battered by ceaseless Nazi air raids.

At that point, Britain was close to bankruptcy. She had no cash to pay for shipping and supplies. FDR came up with one of his "brilliant flashes," as Treasury Secretary Henry Morgenthau put it. Since Britain couldn't pay cash, why not lend or lease her the guns and ships she needed until the war was over?

Roosevelt asked Congress to pass the Lend-Lease Act, which would allow the president to provide war materials to Britain and other nations resisting aggression. Once again, isolationist feelings welled up all over the country. A "Mothers' Crusade" was organized to fight the Lend-Lease bill, and a delegation of mothers knelt in prayer outside the Capitol. In New York, the still-powerful America First Committee staged a

Isolationist members of a "Mothers' Crusade" kneel in prayer outside the Capitol as they urge Congress to kill the Lend-Lease Act.

giant rally in Madison Square Garden to protest the country's growing involvement in the European war.

However, FDR was picking up support. Even Wendell Willkie appeared before a Senate committee to endorse Lend-Lease. When senators reminded him of his campaign charges against Roosevelt, he said, "I struggled as hard as I could to beat Franklin Roosevelt, and I tried to keep from pulling any of my punches. He was elected president. He is my president now."

In March 1941, Lend-Lease was approved overwhelmingly by Congress. By the end of World War II, the United States had provided its allies with some fifty billion dollars' worth of goods and services.

During 1941, Allied fortunes reached a low ebb. In April, Germany occupied Yugoslavia and Greece. In June, Hitler invaded his former ally Russia, and German tanks drove deep into Soviet territory. Meanwhile, Nazi U-boats were prowling the sea-lanes, attacking vessels carrying lend-lease aid to British ports. During the first half of the year, submarines sank 756 Allied ships.

In August, Roosevelt and Churchill met for the first time. For three days, the leaders of the two great English-speaking nations held a series of secret meetings on British and American warships riding at anchor off the coast of Newfoundland, Canada. Out of their conference came a declaration called the Atlantic Charter, which proclaimed self-determination and the "Four Freedoms" – freedom of speech, freedom of religion, freedom from want, and freedom from fear – for all peoples everywhere in the world.

Polls taken that summer showed that three-quarters of all Americans still wanted to stay out of the war in Europe. And yet the country was slipping into an undeclared war in the Atlantic. FDR had ordered American destroyers to escort convoys carrying supplies to Britain and to "shoot on sight" if they encountered Nazi U-boats.

The Atlantic Conference. FDR and Churchill join officers and men in a hymn at religious services aboard the Prince of Wales, *Sunday, August 10, 1941.*

In October, the destroyer *Kearney* was damaged by a torpedo, and eleven crewmen were killed. Later that month, the destroyer *Reuben James* was torpedoed, with the loss of 115 men, becoming the first American vessel sunk by a German submarine. An angry Congress repealed another provision of the Neutrality Act so that American merchant ships could be armed for their own protection. The United States and Germany drifted closer to war.

By now, Nazi tanks were battering at the gates of Moscow. In the Far East, the Japanese had occupied French Indochina (the present Vietnam, Laos, and Cambodia). Japan now posed a threat to the Philippines, an American possession, and to British and Dutch territories in the Far East.

Roosevelt urged Japan to pull out of Indochina. When Tokyo failed to reply, the president issued an executive order cutting off trade between the two countries. In Washington, Secretary of State Cordell Hull began delicate negotiations with Japanese diplomats, hoping to reach an agreement that would insure peace and stability in Asia.

Meanwhile, U.S. Army cryptographers had broken the Japanese diplomatic code. They began to intercept messages hinting that something ominous was about to happen. "War warnings" were sent out to American commanders in the Pacific. To Churchill, FDR cabled: "We must all be prepared for real trouble, possibly soon." But no one expected an attack so close to home.

At dawn on Sunday, December 7, 1941, 350 Japanese dive-bombers, torpedo bombers, and pursuit planes left their aircraft carriers in the Pacific and headed for the American naval base at Pearl Harbor, Hawaii. Caught by surprise, the American Pacific Fleet was almost destroyed. In all, nineteen warships were sunk or damaged and some 265 planes destroyed, most of them while they were still neatly lined up on the ground. More than thirty-five hundred Americans were killed or wounded. Pearl Harbor became the worst naval disaster in American history.

Pearl Harbor, Sunday, December 7, 1941. The U.S.S. West Virginia *and U.S.S.* Tennessee *in flames following the Japanese attack.*

The next day, Roosevelt appeared before a joint session of Congress. Even the isolationists who had so bitterly opposed the president now stood to applaud him as he made his way to the rostrum on the arm of his son James, a captain in the marines. Pearl Harbor had united the American people behind Franklin Delano Roosevelt.

A hushed silence fell over the chamber as he opened the black notebook before him. FDR had worked on this speech until the last minute, adding phrases, substituting words. His face was grave. Reporters could see the whiteness of his knuckles as he gripped the speaker's stand and spoke: "Yesterday, December 7, 1941 – a day which will live in infamy – the United States of America was suddenly and deliberately attacked by naval and air forces of the Empire of Japan. . . ."

The president described in detail what the Japanese had done. When he finished speaking, it took only thirty-three minutes for Congress to declare that a state of war existed between the United States and Japan. That same day in England, both houses of Parliament voted unanimously to declare war on Japan. Three days later, Germany and Italy declared war on the United States.

On December 8, 1941, the president signs a declaration of war with Japan. He wears a black armband to mourn the death of his mother three months before.

Reviewing American troops in North Africa, January 1943. FDR was the first president to leave the United States in wartime.

COMMANDER IN CHIEF

"We have learned to be citizens of the world."
FRANKLIN D. ROOSEVELT

In the dark days following Pearl Harbor, the Allies suffered staggering setbacks all along the vast Pacific front. Japan quickly swallowed the Philippines, Malaya, Burma, and the Dutch East Indies (now Indonesia). Japanese forces pushed far out into the Pacific, occupying the American islands of Guam and Wake, and gaining a foothold in the Aleutians.

In the Atlantic, German U-boats torpedoed and sank hundreds of British and American ships, some even within sight of the Manhattan skyline. On the Russian front, Nazi tanks rumbled through the outskirts of Moscow and Leningrad. And in North Africa, Hitler's troops drove the British back into Egypt and threatened to take the Suez Canal.

Always at his best in an emergency, Roosevelt rose to the occasion as a resolute war leader. He was constantly on the radio, reporting on the war and rallying the American people with the same optimism and determination that had launched the New Deal. Once he declared: "No matter what our enemies . . . in their desperation may attempt to do to us — we will say as the people of London have said, 'We can take it,' and what is more, we can give it back – with compound interest."

FDR took great pride in his new role. At state dinners he preferred to be introduced as "commander in chief" rather than "president." When he learned that Churchill had a top-secret military headquarters, Roosevelt ordered a similar setup in the White House. He called it the Map Room, and he went there every day to receive briefings on all the fighting fronts.

Roosevelt dominated every phase of the war effort. While he did not interfere with day-to-day military operations, he was deeply involved in planning global strategy and long-term diplomatic goals. He insisted that his generals and admirals put their service rivalries aside and work together. On the home front, he called for war production targets that seemed impossible. He would answer protests by saying, "Oh, the production people can do it if they really try!"

"His capacity to inspire and encourage . . . was beyond dispute," said Frances Perkins. "I, and everyone else, came away from an interview with the President feeling better. . . . It wasn't so much what he said as the spirit he conveyed."

As late as 1940, the United States was so poorly prepared for war that soldiers trained with broomsticks for rifles and pieces of cardboard marked "Tank." And yet the nation's factories and shipyards were swiftly harnessed to produce planes, tanks, ships, and weapons. On the president's orders, meanwhile, urgent development of a powerful new weapon went ahead in utmost secrecy at research plants scattered around the country. Few government officials knew anything about the top-secret project. "I can't tell you what this is, Grace," Roosevelt told one of his secretaries, "but if it works, and pray God it does, it will save many American lives."

American war production made it possible for Britain to carry on her struggle against Germany, and for Russia to resist advancing Nazi armies.

"Without American production," said the Soviet leader, Joseph Stalin, "the United Nations could never have won the war." At the same time, the United States mobilized the biggest military force in its history. At peak strength, more than fifteen million men and women were serving in the armed forces.

Unemployment vanished. Because of the manpower shortage, women joined the work force in large numbers to take jobs usually held by men, and "Rosie the Riveter" became a symbol of the war effort. The war also broke down entrenched barriers to the employment of blacks as skilled workers. In 1941, FDR appointed a Fair Employment Practices Committee to enforce his executive order banning discrimination in government and defense industries. Later, Congress passed the Fair Employment Practices Act. It was the first time in the twentieth century that the federal government had tried to enforce civil rights.

The civil rights of the nation's Japanese-Americans did not fare as well. While there was no evidence of espionage or disloyalty among them, they became targets of hysterical prejudice and suspicion. In California, the governor, the attorney general, the state's congressmen, and most of the press demanded that the army evacuate all Japanese residents. "A Jap's a Jap, and I don't want any of them around here," said General John L. DeWitt, head of the West Coast Defense Command.

Early in 1942, Roosevelt gave in to public and military pressure. He signed an order authorizing the internment of 120,000 West Coast Japanese — about half of them American citizens who were deprived of their liberty and branded as disloyal without trial or proof. Forced to sell their homes, farms, and businesses on a week's notice, they were sent to relocation camps in remote desert areas, where they remained until almost the end of the war. (In 1988, the government offered an official apology and compensation of twenty thousand dollars each to surviving Japanese-Americans interned during World War II.)

FDR also has been criticized for not doing enough to help rescue millions of European Jews and other victims of Naziism. The president had expressed his concern on numerous occasions, condemning Nazi crimes and demanding punishment for those responsible. Once the war started, however, he left the refugee problem in the hands of the State Department. It is an unhappy fact that certain high-ranking State Department officials were not sympathetic to the refugees. They claimed that letting down immigration barriers would flood the country with undesirables, such as Communists, criminals, and Nazi spies disguised as refugees. By interpreting the immigration laws strictly, these officials kept many refugees from entering the country. Meanwhile, Congress continued to oppose expanded immigration quotas.

As word of Nazi death camps began to filter out of Europe, State Department officials discredited the reports. The existence of death factories seemed incredible. Most people simply could not imagine that mass murders were taking place. In 1942, when FDR heard about Hitler's plan for the "Final Solution," he at first refused to believe it. And when the reports could no longer be denied, appeals to the Americans and British to bomb the rail lines leading to the camps were rejected by military commanders. They argued that diversions of planes and personnel from bombing military targets would only delay a military victory — the Jews' best chance to survive.

In January 1944, Roosevelt received a confidential report from Treasury Secretary Henry Morgenthau. The report charged that State Department officials "have not only failed to use the Governmental machinery at their disposal to rescue Jews from Hitler, but have even gone so far as to use this Governmental machinery to prevent the rescue of these Jews." The president was finally shocked into action. That week he created the War Refugee Board for the specific purpose of rescuing victims of Naziism. Then he issued a statement that was broadcast all over Europe, printed by underground newspapers, and dropped as leaflets from planes:

Polish Jews from the Warsaw ghetto are marched off to Nazi death camps.

"In one of the blackest crimes in all history — begun by the Nazis in a day of peace and multiplied a hundred times since the war — the wholesale systematic murder of the Jews of Europe goes on unabated at every hour. . . . None who participate in these acts of savagery shall go unpunished. . . . All who share the guilt shall share the punishment."

During the last year of the war, the War Refugee Board saved the lives of more than two hundred thousand Jews and some twenty thousand non-Jews. But if FDR had acted sooner, more of the six million Jews who died might have been saved from the Holocaust.

By the end of 1942 — a year after Pearl Harbor — the tide of battle was beginning to turn. The first Allied naval victories against Japan had been scored that summer in the battles of the Coral Sea and of Midway, where American planes sank three of the same aircraft carriers that had attacked Pearl Harbor. In Russia, the German offensive had stalled at Stalingrad, and the Russians were preparing a massive counterattack. And in North Africa, the British Eighth Army had held fast at Alamein, Egypt, then crashed through Nazi defenses and sent German troops reeling backward with heavy losses.

"Before Alamein we never had a victory," said Winston Churchill. "After Alamein we never had a defeat." In November, two weeks after the battle, two hundred thousand American troops landed at Casablanca in Morocco and at Oran and Algiers in Algeria, trapping Hitler's Afrika Korps between advancing American and British forces.

With the Germans retreating in North Africa, the time had come to plan the next step in the Allied campaign — the invasion of Sicily and the Italian mainland. In January 1943, Roosevelt became the first chief executive to leave the country in wartime, the first to fly, and the first since Lincoln to enter an active war zone when he flew to Casablanca for another meeting with Churchill. At this conference, the two leaders

This giant globe was a gift to the president from the U.S. Army.

announced that "unconditional surrender," rather than a negotiated armistice, would be the sole condition for ending the war.

The year 1943 was one of great international conferences, where Roosevelt and other Allied leaders thrashed out questions of military strategy and postwar peace policy. After Casablanca, Churchill and FDR met again at Washington and at Quebec. Later, they both traveled to Cairo, Egypt, to confer with Chiang Kai-shek, head of the Chinese Nationalist government. By then, China had been fighting the Japanese for six years, suffering its own version of the Holocaust. Millions of Chinese civilians had died in massacres, forced labor projects, and human experiments.

From Cairo, Roosevelt and Churchill went on to Teheran, capital of Iran, for their first "Big Three" conference with the Russian leader, Joseph Stalin. The main topic was the coming Allied invasion of western Europe – the "Second Front" that Stalin had so impatiently demanded.

The Big Three. Meeting for the first time, Stalin, Roosevelt, and Churchill hold a joint press conference at Teheran, Iran, November 29, 1943.

FDR returned from Teheran in a hopeful mood, convinced that the wartime cooperation of the Allies had paved the way for a lasting peace. "Britain, Russia, China, and the United States and their allies represent more than three-quarters of the total population of the earth," he said in a fireside chat. "As long as these four nations with great military power stick together in determination to keep the peace, there will be no possibility of an aggressor nation arising to start another war."

Roosevelt and Churchill met nine times during the war and developed a close personal friendship. On several occasions, the prime minister stayed as a guest at the White House or Hyde Park. FDR would drive Churchill along the familiar roads of the estate in his hand-controlled Ford convertible, speeding recklessly up hills and racing around bends as they left the Secret Service behind. The two leaders also spoke frequently by transatlantic telephone, and they exchanged hundreds of personal messages.

Sharing an army jeep with General Dwight D. Eisenhower, FDR visits American troops in Sicily, December 8, 1943. Eisenhower had just been chosen to command the Allied armies in the coming invasion of Europe.

"I felt the utmost confidence in his upright and inspiring character and outlook," Churchill wrote, "and a personal regard – affection, I must say – for him beyond my power to express. . . ." And Roosevelt once ended a long and serious cablegram to Churchill with the words: "It's fun to be in the same decade with you."

During the war, Eleanor Roosevelt logged more travel miles than the president himself. She visited American troops on three continents, trudging through the mud to see the wounded in military field hospitals. "I met Mrs. Roosevelt at a Navy hospital in New Zealand," one man remembered. "I still recall her pleasant face, her Red Cross uniform, and her walking shoes. She knew what she wanted to see. She took notes on hospital conditions."

By the end of 1943, the Allies were on the offensive in every theater of the war. After chasing the Germans out of Africa, Allied forces occupied Sicily and invaded the Italian mainland. In September, Italy surrendered. Earlier that year, a German army of three hundred thousand had been destroyed at Stalingrad after an epic siege, marking the turning point of the war in Russia. In the Pacific, American troops had taken Guadalcanal from the Japanese in bloody fighting and started their island-hopping advance to Tokyo. And the long-awaited Second Front – the invasion of western Europe – was now scheduled for the spring of 1944.

On D day – June 6, 1944 – Allied forces commanded by General Dwight D. Eisenhower crossed the English Channel and surged onto the beaches of Normandy. More than 150,000 men landed that day, beginning an offensive across France that led to the liberation of Paris on August 25. By then, Russian troops had entered Poland from the east and were advancing toward Warsaw. In the Pacific that summer, the Allies drove the Japanese out of Saipan and Guam, and in October, they landed in the Philippines.

D day, Normandy, France, June 6, 1944. American troops plunge down the ramp of a Coast Guard landing barge and wade ashore through German fire.

Watching for German snipers, American infantry soldiers press on toward Paris, August 1944. Paris was liberated on August 25 after more than four years of German rule.

With victory clearly in sight, another presidential election was approaching. After nearly twelve years in office, Roosevelt showed signs of weariness and ill health. The dark circles under his eyes seemed never to fade. When he lit a cigarette, his hands trembled, and he was wracked by a persistent cough. And yet there was never any doubt that he would run for reelection. "If the people command me to continue in this office and in this war," he said, "I have as little right to withdraw as the soldier has to leave his post in the line."

Meeting in Chicago, the Democrats nominated FDR for a fourth term and Missouri Senator Harry S. Truman as his running mate. The president, meanwhile, was on his way to Pearl Harbor for a meeting with his top commanders in the Pacific, General Douglas MacArthur and Admiral Chester W. Nimitz. Roosevelt's acceptance speech, broadcast from the San Diego naval base, spelled out the themes of his campaign and his goals for the future. "What is the job before us in 1944?" he asked. "First, to win the war – to win the war fast and to win it overpoweringly. Second, to form world-wide international organizations. . . . And third, to build an economy for our returning veterans and for all Americans – which will provide employment and decent standards of living."

FDR's Republican opponent this time was Governor Thomas E. Dewey of New York. The candidates agreed on the conduct of the war and the need for an international organization to prevent future wars. The campaign focused on the fourth-term issue, on the state of the president's health, and on Dewey's charges that "the Communists are seizing control of the New Deal."

To squelch rumors about his health, Roosevelt made campaign appearances in several big cities. One day he drove for hours through New York City in a driving rain, waving gaily from an open car as thousands lined the streets. "I was really worried," said Eleanor, "but instead of being exhausted he was exhilarated."

Never mentioning his opponent by name, Roosevelt dismissed Dewey as "that little man." He promised to continue his New Deal policies after the war, saying, "We are not going to turn back the clock! We are going forward!" And he called for an economic bill of rights – the right to a useful job, a decent home, adequate medical care, and a good education for "all – regardless of station, race, or creed."

FDR won his fourth term by more than 3½ million votes, a tribute to his successful direction of the war effort. He felt that the victory gave him

Reelected to a fourth term, FDR meets the press with Harry Truman (center), his vice-president elect, and Henry Wallace, his outgoing vice-president.

a mandate to end the isolationism of the past and involve America in a world organization that would guarantee a lasting peace.

The inaugural ceremony on January 20, 1945, was brief and simple. Roosevelt had insisted that every one of his thirteen grandchildren come to Washington to see him take the presidential oath one more time. He wore no hat or overcoat as he stood at the lectern in the bitter cold on the south porch of the White House that day. The president spoke for less than five minutes. He looked forward to his next meeting with Churchill and Stalin. "We have learned to be citizens of the world, members of the human community," he said. "We have learned the simple truth, as Emerson said, that 'the only way to have a friend is to be one.'"

Proud grandparents. Eleanor, Franklin, and their thirteen grandchildren pose for a family portrait in the White House on Inauguration Day, January 20, 1945. This was the last family photo taken before FDR's death.

Wounded veterans of World War II listen to the president's fourth inaugural address.

THE ROAD TO PEACE

"I felt as if I knew him."

A SOLDIER

After his fourth inaugural, the president left Washington for another Big Three conference with Churchill and Stalin. Looking haggard and drawn, FDR traveled by sea and air to Yalta, a Russian resort city on the Black Sea. During the journey, he celebrated his sixty-third birthday aboard the American cruiser *Quincy*.

Victory in Europe was almost at hand. Round-the-clock bombing had reduced Berlin to smoking rubble. Except for pockets of last-ditch resistance in Hungary and northern Italy, Hitler's armies had been beaten back onto German soil. In the Pacific, American troops had just liberated Manila, in the Philippines, and B-29s were blasting Japanese cities.

The Yalta Conference was Roosevelt's supreme effort to guarantee a lasting peace with the help and cooperation of the Russians. For eight days in early February, he met with Churchill and Stalin as they discussed the future of Europe, Asia, and the United Nations, a proposed organization designed to assure world peace.

165

Churchill noticed how frail Roosevelt appeared. His face had a "transparency, an air of purification, and often there was a far-away look in his eyes." Yet he managed to shake off his weariness. At the council table, over meals, and in private conversations, FDR seemed to regain some of his old vitality. He was still able to turn on the wit and charm that everyone had come to expect.

Eight days of hard bargaining resulted in a series of compromise agreements that decided the fate of hundreds of millions of people. The outcome was controversial and still affects our world today.

FDR's critics charge that he was outbargained and outsmarted by the wily Russian dictator, that Yalta set the stage for the cold war. The agreements reached there, they say, allowed Stalin to drop an "iron curtain" over half of Europe, making East Germany, Poland, Czechoslovakia, Hungary, and other countries satellites of the Soviet Union.

FDR's defenders say that he and Churchill together made the best deal possible with Stalin. They argue that the cold war resulted not from the Yalta agreements themselves but from Stalin's repeated violations of those agreements.

At the time, Russia's Red Army already occupied most of eastern Europe. Russia had been invaded by Germany twice in a generation, and Stalin was determined to create a buffer zone between his country and the West. Only a World War III could have forced him to give up territory he had won at the cost of millions of Russian lives, and that he considered vital to Soviet security. At Yalta, he promised to allow free elections in eastern Europe. Roosevelt and Churchill took him at his word.

Roosevelt also has been accused of "betraying" China by granting Russia valuable territories in Asia, in return for a Russian declaration of war against Japan. One of FDR's chief goals at Yalta was to get Russia to join the war in the Far East. The atomic bomb was still in the testing stage. The Allied High Command believed that an invasion of the Japa-

Churchill greets a weary FDR as the president arrives in Yalta for another Big Three conference, February 3, 1945.

nese home islands, with perhaps a million Allied casualties, would be necessary to defeat Japan. Roosevelt's generals and admirals told him that a Russian attack on Japan would help shorten the war and save countless American lives.

Roosevelt and Churchill both came away from the conference believing that they had reached a lasting understanding with Stalin. For FDR, the great accomplishment of Yalta was to show the world that the three

The president reports to a joint session of Congress following the Yalta Conference, March 1, 1945.

major powers could cooperate in building the postwar world. And that is the message he carried back to Washington.

He reported on the conference before a joint session of Congress. Now there was no mistaking his ill health. A hush fell over the lawmakers as the president appeared on the floor of the House of Representatives in a wheelchair, something he had never done before. Instead of standing in his braces at the rostrum as he delivered his speech, he sat at a table. And he spoke in a weary and uncertain voice.

"I have come from the Crimean Conference with a firm belief that we have made a good start on the road to peace," Roosevelt said. He reviewed the discussions at Yalta and looked forward to the United Nations Conference to be held in San Francisco that spring, where the UN Charter would be drafted. "Peace can endure only so long as humanity really insists on it, and is willing to work for it, and sacrifice for it," he declared.

Roosevelt was not the same man that Congress and the public had known even months before. Friends who had not seen him for some time were shocked by his appearance. "As soon as I can," he told Vice-President Harry S. Truman, "I will go to Warm Springs for a rest. I can be in trim again if I stay there for two or three weeks."

At the end of March, the president left for the Warm Springs cottage where he had always been able to rest and relax. A few days in the warm Georgia sun revived his spirits and brought color back to his cheeks. He pored over his stamp collection, signed official papers, and worked on the speech he planned to deliver on Thomas Jefferson's birthday, April 13.

The war in Europe was almost over now. Allied troops had crossed the Rhine and swept into western Germany. The Russians were battling on the outskirts of Berlin. In the Pacific, American forces had landed on the island of Okinawa, just three hundred miles from Japan.

On the morning of Thursday, April 12, the president complained of a stiff neck and mild headache when he woke up. Yet his personal physician, Dr. Howard J. Bruenn, thought he looked unusually well. So did FDR's cousins, Laura Delano and Margaret Suckley, who were visiting him at Warm Springs. Another visitor that week was his old friend Lucy Mercer Rutherfurd. Now a widow with grown children, she had kept in touch with Roosevelt over the years. Lucy had come to Warm Springs with the artist Elizabeth Shoumatoff, whom she had commissioned to paint a portrait of the president.

Late that morning, Roosevelt sat at a card table in the living room of his cottage, going over his Jefferson Day speech as Miss Shoumatoff studied him and painted. His guests sat around the room, reading, chatting, and crocheting. A houseboy began to set the table at one end of the living room for lunch. At 12:45, Roosevelt glanced at his watch and announced, "We have fifteen more minutes to work." He lit a cigarette and went back to his speech.

The fifteen minutes were almost up when he pressed his hand to his head. "I have a terrific headache," he said. Then he slumped forward in his armchair. He had suffered a massive cerebral hemorrhage.

Roosevelt never regained consciousness. Carried to his bedroom, he died at 3:35 P.M. central war time. The official announcement of his death listed his name as a war casualty, along with others in the armed services who had given their lives that day: "Army-Navy Dead: ROOSEVELT, Franklin D., Commander-in-Chief, wife, Mrs. Anna Eleanor Roosevelt, the White House."

"On the night he died," Frances Perkins wrote, "a young soldier stood in the silent group which clustered for comfort around the White House where he lived. The young soldier sighed as I nodded to him and, still looking at the house, he said: 'I felt as if I knew him.' (A pause.) 'I felt as if he knew me – and I felt as if he liked me.'"

In Berlin, Joseph Goebbels, the Nazi minister of propaganda, had been telling Hitler that Germany would be saved at the eleventh hour by an unexpected event. When news of Roosevelt's death reached him, he called for champagne and telephoned Hitler, who was barricaded in his underground bunker beneath the flaming ruins of Berlin. "My Führer!" Goebbels announced. "I congratulate you! Roosevelt is dead. It is written in the stars that the second half of April will be the turning point for us. This is Friday the thirteenth of April. It is the turning point!"

On the morning of April 13, a funeral train carrying the president's flag-draped coffin began its slow and mournful journey north from Warm Springs, across the cotton fields of Georgia and the tobacco farms of the Carolinas. Along the way, people stood quietly at every country crossroads and whistle-stop station, waiting to watch the train pass. In towns and cities, the crowds grew bigger. And when the train reached Charlotte, North Carolina, late that night, thousands of people were waiting along the platform and in the streets around the station.

A troop of Boy Scouts began to sing "Onward Christian Soldiers." And then, up and down the station platform and in the streets, other folks joined in. "It started ragged at first, but then it swelled," a reporter wrote. "Soon eight or ten thousand voices were singing like an organ. Those people were scared to death. They weren't singing for a single departed soul. They were singing for themselves, to hold themselves up."

The train arrived in Washington on April 14. A small, black-draped caisson drawn by six white horses carried the coffin from Union Station through streets lined with silent and unmoving crowds – "a processional of terrible simplicity and a march too solemn for tears," wrote William S. White, "except here and there where someone wept alone." As the procession approached the White House grounds, soldiers had to hold back the crowds. Some people knelt on the sidewalk in prayer. A brief service was held in the East Room of the White House.

Citizens in Washington, D.C., mourn as the president's funeral procession passes, April 14, 1945.

The caisson carrying Roosevelt's flag-draped coffin approaches the Capitol.

That night the funeral train left Washington bound for Philadelphia and New York and from there up along the Hudson to Hyde Park. Three of Roosevelt's sons were overseas, but Eleanor and the rest of his family were aboard the train, along with his dog Fala, many of his friends and aides, members of his cabinet, justices of the Supreme Court, eighteen of the reporters who had covered him for so many years, and the new president, Harry Truman, who sat in the armor-plated presidential car with his wife and daughter. Roosevelt's body rode alone in the last car, guarded by four servicemen — army, navy, marine, and coast guard. The train was so long — seventeen cars — and so heavy that at first it would not start. A coupling broke three times before the train pulled out of Washington's Union Station.

It arrived in Hyde Park on the morning of Sunday, April 15. Violets were blooming in the woods where Franklin Roosevelt had hunted birds

FDR's daughter, Anna (left), and his widow, Eleanor, at the president's burial in the Hyde Park rose garden. On the right, partly hidden in the uniform cap, is Roosevelt's son Elliott. His other three sons were overseas.

as a boy, but the branches of the trees were still bare and a cold wind blew off the Hudson. That morning Roosevelt was buried, as he wished, in his mother's rose garden behind the house where he was born.

Two weeks later, on April 30, Adolf Hitler shot himself with his Walther pistol as Russian soldiers closed in on his Berlin bunker. On May 7, Germany's unconditional surrender to the Allies was signed in Berlin.

In August, President Truman made the decision that death had spared Roosevelt from having to make. Truman ordered the dropping of the first atomic bombs on Hiroshima (August 6) and Nagasaki (August 9). On August 14, Japan announced its unconditional surrender, formally signed aboard the U.S. battleship *Missouri* in Tokyo Bay on September 2.

On January 10, 1946, nine months after Roosevelt's death, the first meeting of the United Nations General Assembly opened in London. One of the American delegates was Eleanor Roosevelt. Perhaps she recalled the last words written by her husband, on the eve of his death, in his Jefferson Day speech:

"To you, and to all Americans who dedicate themselves with us to the making of an abiding peace, I say: The only limit to our realization of tomorrow will be our doubts of today. Let us move forward with strong and active faith."

Playing with Elliott on the lawn at Campobello, 1912.

PLACES TO VISIT

Home of Franklin D. Roosevelt National Historic Site, Hyde Park, New York (914) 229-9115. The house where Roosevelt grew up and spent much of his life. Visitors can see the bed Franklin was born in, the birds he collected when he was eleven years old, the special wheelchair he designed for himself, even his wardrobe of clothing and his leg braces. Scattered around his bedroom are the books, magazines, and other items that were there at the time of his last visit in March 1945. Both the president and Mrs. Roosevelt are buried in the family rose garden. Open 9 A.M. to 5 P.M. every day except Christmas and New Year's Day.

Next to the historic site is the *Franklin D. Roosevelt Library and Museum* (914) 229-8114. The museum contains the president's study, his 1936 Ford convertible equipped with special hand controls, his collection of ship models, gifts from foreign rulers, and exhibits about the lives and careers of Franklin and Eleanor Roosevelt. Same hours as the Roosevelt home.

Roosevelt's Little White House and Museum, Warm Springs, Georgia (404) 655-3511. The modest six-room cottage that Roosevelt built for himself as a vacation retreat remains just as it was on the day he died there in 1945. Elizabeth Shoumatoff's unfinished portrait of FDR still stands on its easel in the combination living and dining room where she was painting him on that April afternoon. Open 9 A.M. to 5 P.M. every day except Thanksgiving and Christmas.

Roosevelt Campobello International Park, Campobello Island, New Brunswick, Canada. Write to P.O. Box 97, Lubec, Maine 04652 or P.O. Box 9, Welshpool, New Brunswick EOG 3HO. The thirty-four-room seaside cottage where Franklin was stricken by polio in 1921 contains original furnishings and other items that belonged to the Roosevelt family. Nearby are gardens, picnic areas, and miles of walking trails. At the reception center, visitors can see films on the Roosevelts and on Campobello Island itself. The park opens the Saturday before Memorial Day and remains open for twenty weeks. Visiting hours are 9 A.M. to 5 P.M. seven days a week.

FDR PHOTO ALBUM

*Franklin at age three with his dog,
Budgy, and his pet donkey.*

Springwood, the Roosevelt home at Hyde Park, before the alterations of 1915.

The house at Hyde Park after the 1915 alterations.

Sixteen-year-old Franklin with his dog, Monk.

Franklin and Eleanor on the south porch at Hyde Park, c. 1922.

FDR in his Model A Ford, equipped with special hand controls, c. 1928.

Eleanor, Franklin, and a friend at their Hyde Park swimming pool, c. 1930.

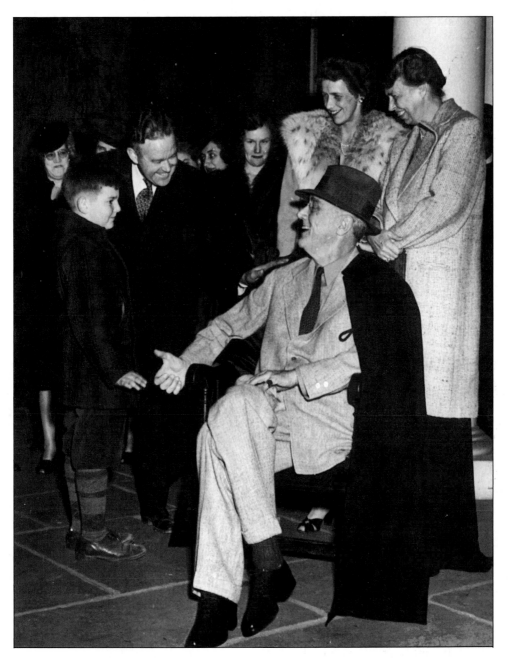

FDR greets his neighbors at Hyde Park on election night, November 7, 1944.

The Roosevelts' summer cottage at Campobello.

Six-year-old Franklin with playmate at the helm of his father's yacht, the Half Moon.

Franklin at eight (center) with some Campobello friends in the scow Merry Chanter.
Climbing the rocks at Campobello, 1902.

*Cruising the Bay of Fundy
on the* Half Moon II, *1904.*

FDR (far right) at Campobello in his sloop, Vireo, *with Anna, James, Elliott, and
four others, 1920.*

On the Amberjack II, *sailing from Marion, Massachusetts, to Campobello, 1933.*

The Little White House, Warm Springs, Georgia.

In the living room at Warm Springs, 1928.

In the pool, c. 1930.

Coming up for air.

Riding at Warm Springs, 1930.

On the porch of the Little White House, 1932.

Greeting a young patient at Warm Springs.

BOOKS ABOUT FDR

"Many books will be written about Franklin Roosevelt, but no two will give the same picture. For no two people saw the same thing in him."

FRANCES PERKINS

Since Frances Perkins made that prediction in 1946, hundreds of books have been written about Franklin Roosevelt. And even today, a half-century after his presidency, Roosevelt's motives, his policies and programs, and the consequences of his acts still inspire controversy.

Roosevelt left no memoirs or autobiography. But he did arrange for the establishment of the nation's first presidential library to house his personal and official papers. Today the Franklin D. Roosevelt Library at Hyde Park, New York, includes a vast collection of books, manuscripts and other documents, photographs, transcripts of interviews, recordings of FDR's speeches, and films. Thousands of scholars and writers have done research in these collections.

For the general reader, two authoritative popular biographies offer detailed accounts of Roosevelt's life and career: Ted Morgan's *FDR: A Biography* (New York, 1985), and Nathan Miller's *FDR: An Intimate History* (New York, 1983). James MacGregor Burns's *Roosevelt: The Lion and the Fox* (New York, 1956) is a classic portrait of FDR as a practical politician, while a second volume by Burns, *Roosevelt: The Sol-*

dier of Freedom (New York, 1970), focuses on the president's role during World War II. Other highly regarded scholarly studies include William E. Leuchtenburg's *Franklin D. Roosevelt and the New Deal, 1932–1940* (New York, 1963); Arthur M. Schlesinger's *The Age of Roosevelt*, 3 volumes (Boston, 1957–60); and Frank B. Freidel's *Franklin D. Roosevelt*, 4 volumes (Boston, 1952–73).

A relatively brief but balanced discussion of Roosevelt's controversial acts and decisions as a war leader can be found in Robert A. Divine's *Roosevelt and World War II* (Baltimore, Md., 1969). Another controversial topic, Roosevelt's record regarding World War II refugees, is discussed by Ronald Sanders in *Shores of Refuge: A Hundred Years of Jewish Emigration* (New York, 1988).

Roosevelt's childhood and youth are the subject of Geoffrey C. Ward's *Before the Trumpet: Young Franklin Roosevelt, 1882–1905* (New York, 1985); a sequel by Ward, *A First-Class Temperament: The Emergence of Franklin Roosevelt* (New York, 1989), continues the story from Roosevelt's honeymoon in 1905 to his election as governor of New York in 1928. For a vivid account of FDR's ordeal with polio, see John Gunther's *Roosevelt in Retrospect: A Profile in History* (New York, 1950).

Joseph Lash, a close family friend, is the author of *Eleanor and Franklin: The Story of Their Relationship, Based on Eleanor Roosevelt's Private Papers* (New York, 1971). Mrs. Roosevelt tells her own story in *The Autobiography of Eleanor Roosevelt* (New York, 1961), which includes material from three earlier volumes of memoirs. Other books by family members include *Affectionately, FDR: A Son's Story of a Lonely Man* by James Roosevelt and Sidney Shalett (New York, 1959), and *An Untold Story: The Roosevelts of Hyde Park* by Elliott Roosevelt and James Brough (New York, 1973).

Among many personal reminiscences by friends and associates, one of the warmest and most revealing is Frances Perkins's *The Roosevelt I Knew* (New York, 1946).

ACKNOWLEDGMENTS AND PICTURE CREDITS

For suggestions, advice, inspiration, and tactical assistance I am grateful to Dorothy Briley, Evans Chan, Michael Cooper, Margery Cuyler, Frank J. Dempsey, James C. Giblin, Isabella Halsted, Curtis Roosevelt, Henry Walter Weiss, and Dr. George Weller. I owe a special debt to Ann Troy, the editor and guiding spirit of this book.

My thanks also to Sylvia Frezzolini, the designer; to the people at the Franklin D. Roosevelt Library at Hyde Park, its director William R. Emerson, its photo archivist Paul McLaughlin, and other members of the staff who helped me select the pictures included here; and to Margaret Roumelis of the National Park Service, who guided me through the Roosevelt home.

All photographs and other illustrations not specifically credited below were furnished by the Franklin D. Roosevelt Library, and are herewith gratefully acknowledged.

The Bettmann Archive: jacket photographs, pages 46, 62, 64, 83, 84, 86, 91, 106, 107, 108, 139, 142, 162, 164, 174.

Library of Congress: pages 34, 44, 76 (both), 78, 79, 90, 93, 100, 104, 121, 123, 124, 141.

National Archives: pages 129, 130, 131, 135, 153.

Wide World Photos: pages 81, 82, 115, 138, 183.

INDEX

Numbers in *italics* refer to pages with illustrations.